BITNET for VMS Users

Michael A. Moore
Ronald M. Sawey

Digital Press

Order number EY-L464E-DP

Printed in the United States of America.

The Publisher offers discounts on bulk orders of this book. For information, please write:

Special Sales Department
Digital Press
One Burlington Woods Drive
Burlington, MA 01003

Service marks, trademarks, and trademarked products mentioned in this book include: American Telephone and Telegraph, AT&T, UNIX; Corporation for Research and Educational Computing, BITNET, CREN, CSNET; Digital Equipment Corporation, the Digital logo, DCL, DEC, DECSystem 10, VAX, VAX/VMS, VAX Notes, VMS, VMSmail; International Business Machines Corporation, IBM, JES2, MVS, NJE, NOTE, Profs, RSCS, TSO, TSO/E, VM, VM/CMS; Joiner Associates Inc., Jnet.

Views expressed in this book are those of the authors, not of the publisher. Digital Equipment Corporation is not responsible for any errors that may appear in this book.

Design: Sandra Calef
Production coordination: Editorial Services of New England, Inc.
Composition: Editorial Services of New England, Inc.
Printing and binding: Maple-Vail Book Manufacturing Group

Library of Congress Cataloging-in-Publication Data
Moore, Michael A.
      BITNET for VMS Users.
      Includes index.
      1. BITNET (Computer network)
I. Sawey, Ronald M. II. Title.
QA76...
ISBN 1-55558-094-7

Contents

Preface

This book is designed to help people interested in computer networks learn about BITNET, a computer network linking many universities and research facilities around the world. It is first a guide for beginners, providing the useful information needed for getting the most out of BITNET. More experienced computer users will appreciate the appendixes, which contain more detailed information about specific programs plus listings of some of the more popular mailing lists, digests, and electronic magazines available via BITNET.

The only tools needed to make full use of this book are 1) an account with network access privileges to BITNET, on a Digital Equipment Corporation VAX computer with the VMS operating system, and 2) instructions for logging on to and off of that computer. All the commands needed for accessing BITNET are contained in this text, along with hands-on examples of these commands. No prior computer experience is assumed, although knowing how the electronic mail and bulletin board programs on your computer work will allow you to proceed at a faster pace. If you're not familiar with even the simplest computer terminology, including words such as *file* and *operating system*, they're explained in footnotes and listed in Appendix A, A Networking Glossary. For those who still feel the need for more introductory material, Appendix B, Recommended Reading, contains a listing of beginner's guides for particular computers and operating systems, plus reference guides to computer networks. If you're still not comfortable with our terminology after reading the first couple of chapters, perhaps some of the books from this list can help you.

Easy access to large computer networks such as BITNET is new to most people. BITNET itself did not start operations until 1981. Southwest Texas State University (SWTSU), where this book was written, was not connected to BITNET until 1986. Only in the past three years were Pan American University (now the University of Texas at Pan American) and Sam Houston State University linked to BITNET, and that was by going through SWTSU. Although military research networks have been in existence for twenty years, access to such global networks has been severely restricted. BITNET has changed that, allowing more and more people the benefits of worldwide communications.

As we move closer to becoming a global village, the authors are glad to have had access to the resources of BITNET for the past five years, and to have watched BITNET more than double in size during that short period. We are deeply indebted to BITNIC, the BITNET Network Information Center, for providing much of the research material that went into this book, and to the SWTSU Computing Services administrators who made access to BITNET possible.

As satisfied users of BITNET, we're proud to be able to heartily recommend BITNET to everyone. The enormous amount of information available via BITNET means there is truly something for everyone, regardless of whether you are interested in the latest (even daily) developments in almost any field imaginable or simply want to relax and enjoy communicating with people sharing your interests.

As authors, we welcome your comments about this book. Although our computer accounts expire annually and have changed numbers innumerable times in past years, we log in daily to check our electronic mail. At present, we may be reached at these addresses:

Michael A. Moore
MMØ2885@SWTEXAS
Logical Designs
PO Box 18328
Austin, TX 78760

Ronald M. Sawey
RSØ1@SWTEXAS
Department of Computer Science
Southwest Texas State University
San Marcos, TX 78666

In conclusion, we wish to thank the many individuals who helped with this book, in particular:

Stephen L. Arnold, Ph.D., Product Manager, Jnet Products, Joiner Associates Inc.

James B. Conklin, Jr., Director, BITNET Network Information Center

Ira Fuchs, founder of BITNET, Vice-President for Computing and Information Technology, Princeton University

Lawrence H. Gindler, Assistant Director for User Services, Trinity University

Tracy LaQuey, author of the *User's Directory of Computer Networks*

Michael E. Meehan, Executive Editor, Digital Press

Don Nash, Networking Systems Specialist, University of Texas System Office of Telecommunication Services

Craig Partridge, Bolt, Beranek & Newman, Palo Alto, CA

Harold Prichett, Systems Programmer, University of Georgia

We also appreciate the support of the faculty, staff, and students at SWTSU who helped with proofreading, checked our examples, and offered suggestions.

Michael A. Moore/Ronald M. Sawey
Spring, 1992

Introduction

What Is a Network?

With computers, the term *network* refers to two or more computers linked together to exchange data. A network may be as simple as two computers with wires running between them, or as complex as thousands of computers connected via direct cables, dial-up phone lines, and microwave transmitters/receivers. Networks exist for one primary purpose: to facilitate the exchange of data between computers. People using one computer invariably want access to information on another computer, or they want to communicate with someone using another computer. Networks provide the communications ability needed to transmit information from one computer to another.

A small network, typically linking computers in the same room or building, is called a *local area network,* or *LAN.* A network that links computers (and other networks) at different sites is a *wide area network,* or *WAN.* It is very common for a WAN to be used to link LANs together.

What Is BITNET?

On one hand, BITNET is a wide area network linking computers at universities in the United States and Mexico. It is administered both locally and nationally. On the other hand, BITNET is a logical network connecting over 3000 computers at more than 1300 academic and research sites around the world. It is made up of many organizations jointly cooperating to provide network services. Two of the most well known members of the logical BITNET network are the NetNorth network in Canada and EARN (the European Academic Research Network) overseas. Many state and regional networks are also a part of BITNET, as are other networks in countries around the world.

The U.S. and Mexican portion of BITNET is administered by a non-profit organization, the Corporation for Research and Educational Networking (CREN), founded to help "connect all the scholars of the world." BITNET links scholars via interactive messages, file transfers, and electronic mail, all explained in detail later. Computer users at any two BITNET sites have the capability to communicate directly with each other even though they may be thousands of miles apart. The **SEND** program allows anything typed at one computer to be almost instantly transmitted to another computer and displayed. Electronic mail may be transferred back and forth with ease, even being temporarily stored at sites along the way and later forwarded, if transmission problems cause interference. Automated user directory servers, list servers, and database servers allow information on other computers to be made available locally. Thus, BITNET provides both a strong and flexible platform for use in communicating with other computer users and accessing other computers.

How This Book Can Help You

Accessing the services BITNET provides, from each of the different types of computers connected to BITNET, can be a real problem. The electronic mail, news, and communications programs from various vendors may be similar, but the commands to access them are often just different enough to confuse people. Also, each of the computer gateways used to link BITNET to other networks has idiosyncrasies that puzzle even networking experts.

This book is the solution for people using Digital Equipment Corporation VAX computers with the VMS operating system and Joiner Associates Inc. Jnet software for accessing BITNET. Even if you don't have a VAX/VMS computer, the commands used on your particular computer are probably similar to the VMS commands, so this book may still be helpful to you. Also, in places, commands for other computers are noted.

This book is organized into seven chapters, with each chapter discussing a particular aspect of BITNET. Appendixes provide a more detailed look at specific programs and commands, plus list sources for additional information available via BITNET.

Chapter 1, BITNET History and Organization, traces the roots of BITNET, explains how it is administered, and gives the purpose and goals behind BITNET. Included is a summary of what BITNET can do for you, along with a discussion of BITNET rules.

Chapters 2–4 each discusses one of the major services available via BITNET and shows how to best take advantage of that service. They go together with Chapter 5, Servers, which provides details on some of BITNET's most widely used, but least understood, services— automated servers that process your commands. Beginners should pay particular attention here; these four chapters discuss the very heart of BITNET. They should also be read in order; each chapter builds on the commands and terminology learned in the previous chapter.

Chapter 6, Gateways to Other Networks, discusses other computer networks and how BITNET connects to them. Sending mail to people on other networks and getting a reply can be complicated.

Chapter 7, The Future of BITNET, concludes with an essay on what the future might hold for BITNET and how planned improvements will make it a premier network for students and researchers in the future.

Finally, the appendixes provide the additional support you will
need to continue exploring BITNET, including a glossary of network
terminology. Several appendixes contain network addresses and
descriptions of the most popular and useful list servers, database
servers, and user directory servers.

BITNET History and Organization

1.1

"Because It's Time"

BITNET began in May 1981. Ira Fuchs, then Vice Chancellor for the City University of New York (CUNY), saw IBM's internal mail network, VNET, and determined a need existed for a similar low cost, easy-to-use network for Eastern U.S. and Canadian universities. Fuchs collaborated with Greydon Freeman, then director of the Yale Computing Center, to link IBM mainframe computers[1] on their campuses and thus created BITNET. In the first year, BITNET connected six universities; the next year the total was up to twenty, including the University of California at Berkeley on the West Coast. As of January 1991, the "Because It's Time"[2] network had grown to connect 3300 computers at more than 1300 sites around the world. BITNET also has connections, called *gateways*, to other major computer networks such

---

1. Computers are divided into various classes according to many factors, including processing power and number of simultaneous users. Generally, a computer that supports one user is a microcomputer or workstation. A larger computer, supporting anywhere from two users to three hundred users, is often considered a minicomputer. A still larger and more powerful computer, typically handling hundreds of users, is called a mainframe.

2. BITNET is also sometimes called the "Because It's There" network.

as the Internet, UUCP, and FidoNet. These gateways allow electronic mail to be exchanged.

Originally, BITNET was a single computer network connecting sites across the United States. It is now a *logical* network or *meta-network* encompassing other networks around the world. It has many interconnections, but each network is separately administered. The portion of BITNET in the United States and Mexico is simply called *BITNET.* In Europe, BITNET is known as *EARN,* the European Academic and Research Network, while the Canadian portion of BITNET is called *NetNorth.*

EARN began as an IBM proposal in 1982 to link more than 60 universities and academic research centers in Europe. IBM's proposal was accepted in 1984; EARN was linked to BITNET in the United States with a line from Rome, Italy to New York City. EARN now has over 750 computers networked together in 24 countries in Europe, the Middle East, and Africa.

NetNorth, the Canadian portion of BITNET, began as an agreement between eight Ontario universities in 1983. Originally called *OUNET* (Ontario University Network), it started operations in 1984, connecting eight IBM mainframes. IBM Canada financed much of the growth of NetNorth, although member universities now pay most network costs. In 1985, the University of Guelph in Ontario was linked to Cornell University in the United States, making NetNorth officially a part of BITNET.

BITNET reaches around the world with additional networks, such as CAREN (Japan, Taiwan, Korea), GulfNet (Persian Gulf countries), ANSP (Brazil), RUNCOL (Colombia), and others. BITNET is constantly changing, with more computers and more networks being added every year. Maps and listings of the computers and networks that make up BITNET are available in electronic form at many different sites. Figure 1.1 shows a map of BITNET and its connections around the world.

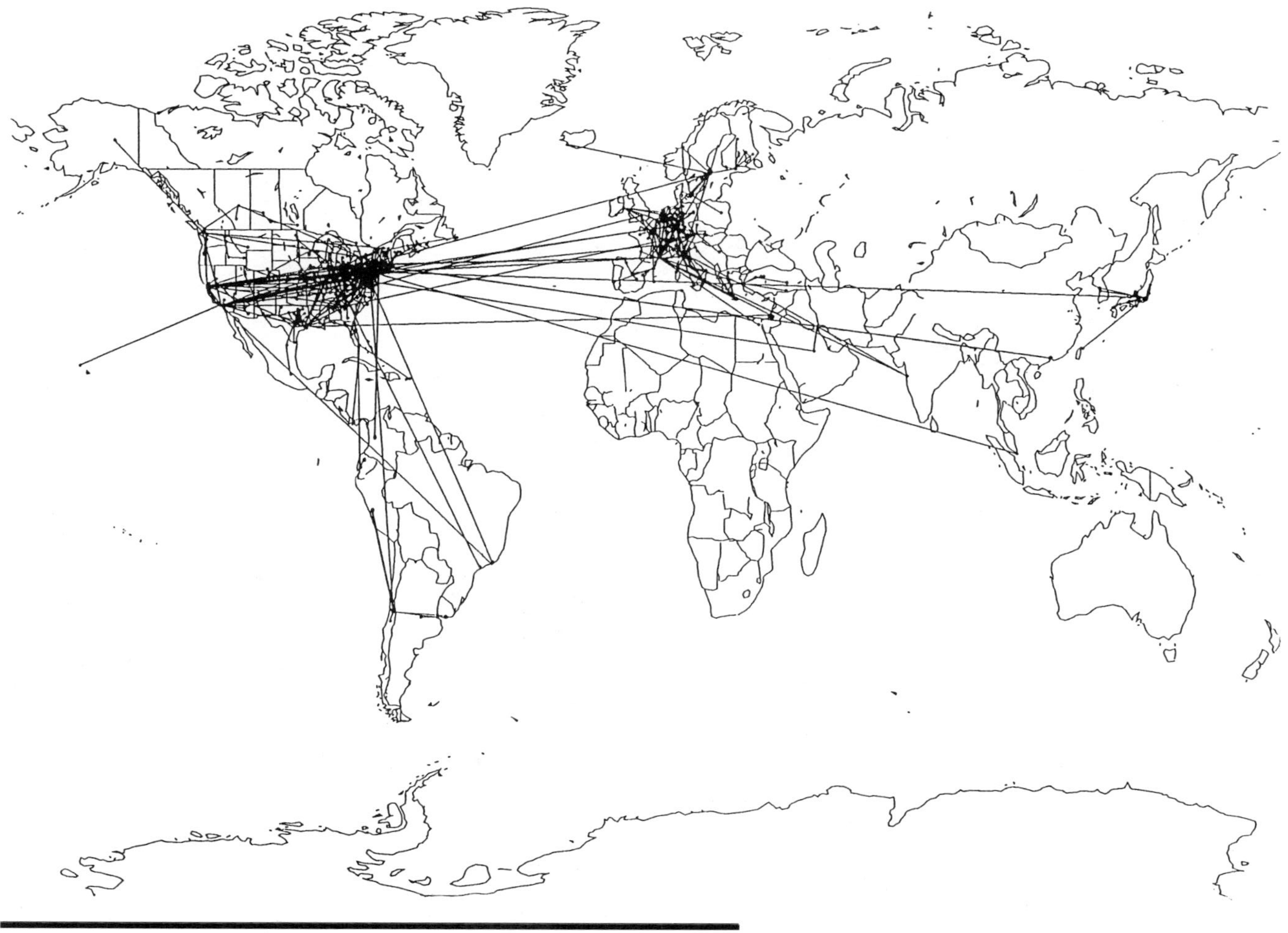

Figure 1.1   BITNET Connections Around the World

To understand the structure of BITNET and how individual computers are linked to form the network, some computer terminology is helpful. The pattern of connections in a computer network is called its *topology*. At one time, BITNET was a *spanning tree network*. A spanning tree looks like it sounds—a tree with branches spreading out from a single trunk, with each branch splitting into two or more other branches. Spanning means that there is only one route between any two branches; there are no loops. A single computer is thought of as the root of the tree. For BITNET, the City University of New York (CUNY), was the *root node*.[3]

The problem with having a single root node was that most network traffic passed through the node, in this case creating a bottleneck not only at CUNY but also at the nodes connecting directly to it. As a solution to this problem, a proposal was adopted in 1989 that reorganized BITNET into regions. Two computers in each region serve as root nodes for the region. This ring of root nodes is connected to each other via high-speed data lines, much faster than typical BITNET links. These nodes now carry the bulk of traffic, forming a high-speed *backbone* for BITNET.

Directly above each root node are other BITNET nodes, some still organized as trees. Figure 1.2 shows the portion of BITNET that includes Southwest Texas State University. This form allows messages to travel down the tree only as far as needed to get to another branch of the tree. If the node the message is trying to reach is in another tree, the message has to go all the way down the tree to a root node, get passed to another root node, then go up another tree. Although this organization is efficient, guaranteeing that only a minimum number of nodes will have to be traversed to reach any other node, the failure of a single node can cause every node above it to be cut off from communication. Thus, there are also some lateral connections, allowing a nonfunctioning node to be bypassed. Nodes directly above the regional root nodes are arranged so that any root node failure will not cut off

---

3. With computer networks, the term *node* refers to a logical connection on a network. A *root node* is the node to which all other computers ultimately connect.

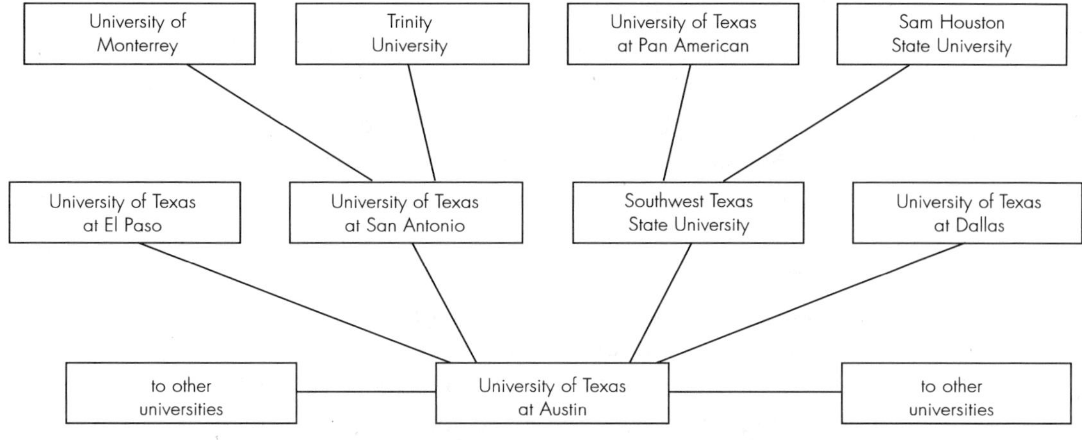

Figure 1.2 BITNET Topology Showing Southwest Texas

other nodes in a region. One of the requirements for joining BITNET as a full member is that at least one other node be allowed to link to your site; many universities cooperate further, allowing two or more connections. As of May 1989, there were 22 direct links to CUNY, including those going overseas and to other network gateways. Other root nodes also have a large number of connections.

1.3 *BITNET Networking Protocols*

BITNET began as a network of IBM mainframes using IBM's Remote Spooling Communications Subsystem (RSCS) software. RSCS is a privileged program that runs under the IBM VM operating system[4] and allows computers to be linked in a network without additional software. RSCS implements the Network Job Entry (NJE) protocol,[5] which is also available for other IBM computers and operating systems, making connections between different IBM mainframes

---

4. An *operating system* is special software used to control computer hardware; it allows peripherals, such as printers, disk drives, and terminals, to communicate with each other and to be controlled by a computer user. *VM* is one of IBM's mainframe operating systems in widespread use on BITNET.

5. A *protocol* defines how processes communicate with each other. For example, with computer communications, at times one computer must listen to instructions while at other times it must give instructions. A protocol determines who's allowed to talk and who must listen under various conditions.

possible. Thus, BITNET expanded rapidly to any site with an IBM mainframe computer.

In 1982, Penn State University (PSU) developed UREP (UNIX RSCS Emulation Program) software that allowed computers running the UNIX[6] operating system to communicate using IBM NJE protocols. An NJE implementation for Digital VAX computers running the VMS[7] operating system was also written at PSU. It was later purchased by Joiner Associates Inc. and called *Jnet.* Other major computer manufacturers, including Prime, Control Data Corporation (CDC), and Burroughs (now Unisys) also developed software for emulating NJE so that their computers could connect to BITNET. Now, about 30% of BITNET sites use IBM mainframes; VAX computers running the VMS operating system represent 44% of the nodes, with another 11% using computers from various vendors that use the UNIX operating system.

The NJE protocol makes BITNET a "store and forward" network. Information (in the form of a file) going from one site to another may have many intermediate nodes to pass through; to complete this path, a file is passed in its entirety from one node to the next before continuing on. If a connection is down between two nodes, files are stored until the connection has been restored.

In 1986, the BITNET II project was started at Princeton University by Ira Fuchs out of concern for the cost of the dedicated communications lines required by BITNET and by the technological speed limits of such lines. Other major computer networks use the Internet Protocol suite, commonly called *TCP/IP* (for Transmission Control Protocol and Internet Protocol, two of the most well known of the Internet protocols). The BITNET II project has made it possible to communicate over TCP/IP networks and at higher speeds. The NJE protocol that forms the basis for BITNET communications does not control the underlying speed of BITNET, which is a function of lower level protocols. When

---

6. *UNIX* is a minicomputer operating system originally developed at Bell Labs for American Telephone and Telegraph (AT&T) but now in widespread use.

7. *VMS* is a proprietary operating system for Digital Equipment Corporation VAX minicomputers. (It is not the same as VM or MVS, which are proprietary IBM operating systems.)

BITNET was started, the fastest of the low-level protocols that would work with RSCS could communicate at a speed no greater than 19,200 bits per second (bps).[8] To get around this limitation, a program for sending NJE data over TCP/IP networks (VMNET) was developed for IBM mainframes as part of the BITNET II project; it allows a speed of 1.5 million bps, with 100 million bps planned for the future. Enhancements to Jnet and UREP were also developed to support BITNET II.

1.4   *BITNET Administration*

In September 1989, BITNET administratively merged with CSNET, a 145 member network sponsored by Computer Science departments at universities around the world. The merger allowed the two networks to combine their separate legal and administrative operations. CREN, the Corporation for Research and Educational Networking, was created to replace BITNET, Inc., the previous trustees for BITNET. A combined board of trustees with 12 members was appointed to CREN from CSNET and BITNET. Two years later, CSNET services were discontinued because increased competition from other networks caused a drop in demand for CSNET services.

Under the CREN bylaws, BITNET member sites are required to provide a single representative:

- A *CREN Member Representative* is a senior-level manager or administrator appointed by the member institution's president or chancellor. The Member Representative represents the institution on policy and financial manners, appoints any other CREN representatives, and votes for the institution.

The CREN Member Representative may optionally appoint three other representatives to handle particular aspects of being a BITNET site:

- A *Technical Representative* oversees local technical matters such as the BITNET routing tables, database management, and mailer operations.

---

8. A *bit* is the smallest possible piece of data, often thought of as either a one or a zero or as representing an on or off state. A *byte* is a combination of bits, typically seven or eight; single characters are usually thought of as one byte of data each.

- An *Information Services Representative* provides local information services support, communicating BITNET access information and answering user questions.
- A *Billing Agent* handles financial matters between the institution and CREN.

A formal structure for BITNET was not defined until 1984, when it became obvious that rapid growth was presenting problems. A three-year grant from IBM led to the establishment of a Network Information Center (BITNIC) at EDUCOM[9] and a Development and Operations Center (BITDOC) at CUNY.

With BITNET's formal structure also came a need to be self-sufficient. User fees were implemented in 1987. Current fees are $750–$10,000 annually for nonprofit institutions and $2,000–$25,000 annually for profit organizations.

<table>
<tr><td>**1.5**</td><td>

Network Rules

</td></tr>
</table>

Network Rules

CREN sets requirements for both membership in CREN and BITNET access. There are limitations on who may access BITNET, technical requirements for connecting to BITNET, and guidelines to follow once access is given. Enforcement is generally left up to the CREN and BITNET representatives at each site and to anyone providing a specific service, such as someone acting as a moderator for a mailing list. If a site is having trouble with someone from a different node, a message sent to one of the representatives at the offender's node will usually clear up problems. The CREN board of trustees also has the authority to revoke BITNET memberships. Mailing list moderators have also been known to reject messages from people not following their *posting*[10] rules.

---

9. EDUCOM is a consortium of universities, colleges, and other institutions formed in 1964 to "facilitate the introduction, use, and management of information technologies." A group of 40 research institutions make up the EDUCOM Networking and Telecommunications Task force, which works "to support the development of computer networking technology." EDUCOM now has 530 universities and colleges as. members plus 95 corporations as associate members.

10. In this case, *posting* refers to making information available to other people via a mailing list or bulletin board. Just as sheets of paper are posted on traditional bulletin boards, electronic messages are posted on electronic bulletin boards.

Faculty, staff, and students at institutions that are CREN members are normally eligible for access to BITNET. Individual faculty at non-member institutions are eligible for guest access, but most other access to BITNET requires written authorization from CREN. BITNET sites also require permission from CREN to provide connections between BITNET and other networks, with some exceptions.

From a technical standpoint, CREN requires each BITNET site to connect to another site via a 9600 bps or faster connection and support the RSCS/NJE networking protocols. The computer with the BITNET connection must also operate 20 hours a day, 7 days a week, and pass all messages and files through to other BITNET sites without charge.

CREN provides guidelines for use of BITNET and CSNET via an Acceptable Use Policy.[11] This policy, available from CREN, states:

> Use of CREN networks shall:
>
> > Be consistent with the purposes of and goals of the networks
> >
> > Avoid interfering with the work of other users of the networks
> >
> > Avoid disrupting the network host systems (nodes)
> >
> > Avoid disrupting network services

The policy also gives specific examples of acceptable and unacceptable network usage:

> Messages that are likely to result in the loss of recipients' work or systems are prohibited.
>
> CREN networks are not to be used for commercial purposes, such as marketing, reselling bandwidth, or business transactions between commercial organizations.
>
> Advertising is forbidden. Discussion of a product's relative advantages and disadvantages by users of the product is encouraged. Vendors may respond to questions about their products as long as the responses are not in the nature of advertising.

---

11. To get a copy of this policy, request the file CREN NET_USE from LISTSERV@BIT-NIC. The file NETINFO FILELIST contains a listing of other files about CREN and BITNET. *See* Chapter 5, Servers, for information on how to retrieve files from a LISTSERV.

CREN networks may be used for the provision of services which support the needs and purposes of the CREN networks, and for which a charge is made, if the network is an optional mechanism for provision of this service for which no additional charge is made, and as long as the use of the service is consistent with the bandwidth of the networks and the forwarding hosts. Providers of such information may be nonprofit or for profit organizations.

Any communication which violates applicable laws and regulations is not allowed.

"Chain letters," "broadcasting" messages to lists of individuals, and other types of use which would cause congestion of the networks or otherwise interfere with the works of others are not allowed.

BITNET files will be limited to sizes determined and reviewed periodically. (Note: The current limit is 300,000 bytes per file transmitted.)

Federal and state laws also apply to BITNET usage. Accessing a computer without permission, destroying someone else's computer data, and intercepting or reading electronic mail for another computer user all violate the Electronic Privacy Act of 1986. If done for commercial purposes, any one of these violations may result in up to a $250,000 fine and a year in jail; or, if done for noncommercial purposes, up to a $5,000 fine and six months in jail. Some states have similar laws; Texas law makes it a crime to give your computer password to someone else without the system administrator's permission; both you and the person receiving the password can be prosecuted. Posting of copyrighted material may also violate federal copyright laws (Title 17, U.S. Code); although educational use of copyrighted material is sometimes permitted, it is better to post with the permission of the author and copyright owner.

Individual countries also have regulations concerning the exportation of technology, which includes files and messages. For example, any material sent out of the United States must satisfy the Department of Commerce General Technical Data Availability (GTDA) policy[12] or

---

12. Three files detailing the GTDA policy and how it relates to BITNET are available from LISTSERV@BITNIC as LEGAL COUNSEL, LEGAL GTDA, and LEGAL COMMERCE. *See* Chapter 5, Servers, for information on how to retrieve files from a LISTSERV.

have an export license. This is not usually a concern for most BITNET users, but it has limited the distribution of a popular file compression program due to the program using an algorithm for data encryption that is covered under the GTDA policy.

1.6 BITNET Services

BITNET provides three methods of communicating via computers: interactive messages, file transfers, and electronic mail. These communications methods make it possible for many types of services to be offered via BITNET, and they may be combined when offering services. Servers, an important part of BITNET, often combine interactive messages, files transfers, and electronic mail to provide worldwide access to information at specific sites.

Interactive messages up to 160 characters in length may be sent between any two people logged onto computers connected to BITNET. For the most part, messages are transmitted almost instantaneously; if people are logged onto nodes that are far apart, a short transmission delay may take place, although a delay of more than a minute is very unusual. Messages may also be transmitted between a person logged on and a program running on another node. Chapter 2, Interactive Messages, explains interactive messages in detail.

BITNET allows *file transfers*, the sending and receiving of data stored in files, from one person to another. Because of network congestion, BITNET policy states that only files of less than 300,000 bytes in size be transmitted, although the network is capable of sending much larger files. Specialized *list server* programs send files in response to interactive messages and electronic mail sent by computer users. Chapter 3, File Transfers, explains how files may be transferred from one BITNET node to another.

Electronic mail, commonly called *e-mail*, is similar to paper mail; a message from one person is written, addressed, and mailed to someone with an account on another computer. The other person does not have to be logged on to receive mail; messages are stored automatically. As with interactive messages, mail may be sent to programs that interpret the instructions in the mail message and act on them. Mail may also be addressed to more than one person at a time; BITNET sends copies to each person. Electronic mail is often used with mail distribution lists; a message sent to a particular location is rebroadcast to all users that are members of that mailing list. Hundreds of mailing lists are available, on a wide variety of topics. *See* Chapter 4, Electronic Mail, for more information on e-mail.

Using these methods of communication, thousands of services are available via BITNET. User directory servers allow people to register their names with central databases so that other computer users may look up their network addresses. There are network commands to find out the status of a particular computer, even showing who is logged onto it. A variety of electronic magazines are distributed via BITNET, along with digests (collections of mail messages) and mailing lists on many popular topics. Relay servers allow communications between people on different nodes, similar to a telephone conference call. Some services are a little unusual but fulfill a need; for example, a poetry server exists to send poems to people who request them, and a mailing list even exists for "deadheads," people who are fans of the rock group, The Grateful Dead. Chapter 5, Servers, describes the various types of servers, and the appendixes include lists of services available via BITNET.

Chapter 2

Interactive Messages

BITNET allows short messages to be sent between two people who are using computers at the same time. Such *interactive messages,* also known as *real-time messages,* may be up to 160 characters long. They travel very quickly through BITNET and receive priority over file transfers because of their small size. When sender and receiver are on nodes close to each other or on the same node, transmission is almost instantaneous. When nodes are far apart, a short delay may be experienced, typically no more than a minute but actually depending on the amount and type of other network traffic.

Sometimes interactive messages are sent to programs running on other computers. These messages are commands to perform a specific task, such as to list the user names of people currently logged on, or to provide statistics on computer usage.

2.1   Sending Messages

The command used to send interactive messages is what you might expect: **SEND**.[1] Using **SEND** is similar to having a phone conversation.

---

1. While **SEND** is standard on VAX/VMS systems, other computer operating systems may use different commands. IBM VM/CMS systems use the **TELL** command,

First you need to know the area code (node name) and phone number (user name) of the person you're calling. Then the person must be home (logged on) when you call. The simplest case of using **SEND** is when the person being called is in the same area code (on the same node) as you are, so you only need to know his/her local phone number (user name):

```
SEND user "message"
```

The word *user* refers to the user name of a person who is logged on; *message* is up to 132 characters[2] of text, enclosed by double quotes. The quotes are required to prevent the VMS operating system from converting your message to all uppercase letters. VMS also interprets anything after an exclamation mark (!) as a comment and does not send it. Apostrophes (') also have special meanings with VMS and should not be used without double quotes around the message.

When sender and receiver are logged on to different computers, the sender must know what node the receiver is using and include it with the **SEND** command:

```
SEND user@node "message"[3]
```

Another method is to define a *nickname* or *alias* that includes both the node and user names. The nickname may then be used in place of both the node and user names when sending. The VAX/VMS operating system **DEFINE** command allows this:

```
DEFINE nickname "user@node"
```

If such nicknames are put in a file called **LOGIN.COM**, they will be available for use each time you log in.

When an interactive message arrives, a bell sounds and the message appears on the terminal of the person to whom the message is sent. There are the following exceptions:

---

while IBM MVS systems with TSO/E may use **TRANSMIT** or **XMIT**. IBM MVS systems with JES2 may use **TO**, **VMSG**, or **XMSG**.

2. The limitation for BITNET characters is 160 per line. For a VAX computer with VMS the limitation is 132 characters per line.

3. **TELL user AT node** is the syntax for IBM VM/CMS systems.

1. The receiver is not logged on.
2. The receiver has turned off broadcast messages (by using an operating system command).
3. The receiver is using a program that rejects messages or captures them without immediately displaying them.

An error message is usually displayed on the screen of the sender when a message does not reach a receiver. The most common messages warn that a receiver is not logged on, a receiver has the terminal set to reject messages, or a link is down between sender and receiver preventing the message from reaching its destination.

Another form of the **SEND** command makes communicating back and forth between two people much like a phone conversation. By not specifying a message to send, you're prompted repeatedly for text, until a blank line is entered. For example:

```
$ SEND user@node
(node)user: Text for the receiver may be typed here and
(node)user: here until an empty (blank) line is entered. Lines are sent
(node)user: one at a time. Up to 160 characters may be transmitted
(node)user: interactively at a time via BITNET, although different
(node)user: implementations of SEND may impose lower limits, and
(node)user: truncate text!
(node)user:
```

The *(node)user:* prompt displays the node and user name of the person to whom you are sending a message. This form of the **SEND** command makes it much easier to send messages because the sender's node name and user name only have to be entered once.

Quotes are not required around text entered using this form of **SEND**. However, if a dollar sign ($) is entered as the first character on a line, it is a signal to interpret the text on that line as a command to the operating system on your node, rather than as text to send.

If a receiver sends messages back, they appear on the sender's screen, allowing a two way conversation. Figure 2.1 shows **SEND** being used by two people to communicate with each other. A group conversation is also possible via **RELAY**, which is described in Chapter 5, Servers.

```
$ SEND SMITH@UTADNX
(UTADNX)SMITH: Joe, are you busy?
        (UTADNX)SMITH - Not at all.  What do you need?
(UTADNX)SMITH: What is the BITNET node name for SWT?
        (UTADNX)SMITH - SWTEXAS.
(UTADNX)SMITH: Thanks, bye.
```

Figure 2.1 Having a Conversation Using SEND

2.2   *Sending Commands*

SEND is not limited to communications between people; it may also be used to issue commands to programs running on other computers. For commands sent to IBM VM/CMS mainframes, the **CPQUERY** and **QUERY** commands are available. For sending to VAX/VMS systems, **HELP** and **SHOW** may also be allowed.[4] **CPQUERY** and **QUERY** are IBM RSCS/NJE commands that return a wide variety of information about processes running on a node. It is possible to use them to discover who is logged onto a node, and to get disk storage and processor statistics. **SHOW** works similarly for VAX/VMS systems, presenting information in a format more familiar to VAX/VMS users. **HELP** displays information about **SEND** and how it may be used.

Some of the more useful commands, **CPQUERY INDICATE**, **CPQUERY NAMES**, and **SHOW USERS** are described here. Although the full spellings of commands are listed in the examples used here, abbreviations are also permitted. For example, **CPQUERY INDICATE** may be abbreviated to **CPQ IND**, or even **CP I. SHOW USERS** is often abbreviated as **SH U.** Commands also do not have to be typed in quotes to preserve upper-case and lowercase letters.

2.2.1   *CPQUERY INDICATE*

CPQUERY INDICATE (Figure 2.2) displays node status information. On VAX/VMS nodes, the type of computer and operating system, the date

---

4. Some sites disable **QUERY, SHOW,** and **HELP** commands for increased system security, thus preventing other people from knowing who is logged onto their computers and keeping them from knowing what commands are available. Also, due to the various implementations of these commands, output from them varies from one system to the next.

```
$ SEND @SWTNYSSA CPQUERY INDICATE                          (VAX/VMS to other VAX/VMS)
(SWTNYSSA) - VAX 8650 running VAX/VMS V5.2
(SWTNYSSA) - Up since 27-SEP-1989 18:05
(SWTNYSSA) - Member of Jnet cluster SWTEXAS


$ SEND @TAMVM1 CPQUERY INDICATE                              (VAX/VMS to IBM VM/CMS)
(TAMVM1) - CPQ: CPU   - 100%  APU   - 000%  Q1-02  Q2-03  STORAGE-034%  EXPAN-007
(TAMVM1) - CPQ: PAGING-0004/SEC  STEAL-001%  LOAD-000%  SWAPPING-0000/SEC


$ SEND @SWTEXAS %CPQUERY INDICATE                           (VAX/VMS to a VAXcluster)
(SWTNYSSA) - VAX 8650 running VAX/VMS V5.2
(SWTNYSSA) - Up since 27-SEP-1989 18:05
(SWTNYSSA) - Member of Jnet cluster SWTEXAS
(SWTTEGAN) - VAX 8650 running VAX/VMS V5.2
(SWTTEGAN) - Up since  28-SEP-1989 10:05
(SWTTEGAN) - Member of Jnet cluster SWTEXAS
```

Figure 2.2 Querying CPU Information

and time the computer was last restarted, and the VAXcluster [5] name
for the computer are indicated. For IBM mainframe nodes, central
processor usage and disk storage statistics are displayed.

The **CPQUERY INDICATE** command has this syntax:

```
SEND @node CPQUERY INDICATE
```

Commands may be sent to all computers in a VAXcluster. **CPQUERY
INDICATE** can run for all computers in a VAXcluster by using the cluster
name and preceding the **CPQUERY** command with a percent (%) sign:

```
SEND @cluster %CPQUERY INDICATE
```

2.2.2   *SHOW USERS and CPQUERY NAMES*

SHOW USERS lists the user name of each person currently logged on to
a VAX/VMS node, along with the name of the program running, how
long the user has been logged on, the amount of central processor time
used, and an identification code to indicate the terminal being used.

---

5. DEC connects VAX computers in groups called *VAXclusters*. Computers so
grouped may be referred to either individually or by a single name. For example,
SWTEXAS is the VAXcluster name for two computers, SWTNYSSA and SWTTEGAN.

```
$ SEND @SWTNYSSA QUERY SYSTEM                                    (VAX/VMS to other VAX/VMS)
(SWTNYSSA) - Link SWTTEGAN Connect   -- DT  Line TEGAN    NOH NOD NOT
(SWTNYSSA) - Link UTGATE   Connect   -- DT  Line UTGATE   NOH NOD NOT
(SWTNYSSA) - Link SHSUODIN Connect   -- DT  Line ODIN     NOH NOD NOT
(SWTNYSSA) - Link PANAM2   Connect   -- DT  Line PANAM2   NOH NOD NOT


$ SEND @TAMVM1 QUERY SYSTEM                                      (VAX/VMS to IBM VM/CMS)
(TAMVM1) - LINK SFAUSTIN CONNECT -- BITSML LINE 0D1 NOH NOD NOT
(TAMVM1) - LINK TAMVENUS CONNECT -- BITVMB LINE 0C5 NOH NOD NOT
(TAMVM1) - LINK TAMUNIX CONNECT -- DMTVMC LINE 200 NOH NOD NOT
(TAMVM1) - LINK TAMMVS1 CONNECT -- JESNJI LINE 418 NOH NOD NOT
(TAMVM1) - LINK TAMCBA CONNECT -- DMTVMH LINE 0C4 NOH NOD NOT
(TAMVM1) - LINK VM1SNA CONNECT -- BITNJI LINE 300 NOH NOD NOT
(TAMVM1) - LINK TAMVM2 INACTIVE -- DEFAULT DMTVMC LINE 500


$ SEND @SWTNYSSA QUERY SYSTEM SUM                                (VAX/VMS to other VAX/VMS)
(SWTNYSSA) - Link SWTTEGAN line activity: TOT=2270; ERRS=0; TMOUTS=0
(SWTNYSSA) - Link UTGATE   line activity: TOT=46699; ERRS=0; TMOUTS=0
(SWTNYSSA) - Link SHSUODIN line activity: TOT=9927; ERRS=0; TMOUTS=0
(SWTNYSSA) - Link PANAM2   line activity: TOT=29218; ERRS=0; TMOUTS=0
```

Figure 2.3 Using QUERY SYSTEM to See Connections

CPQUERY NAMES works similarly, but it displays only the user name and terminal of each person. Some sites discourage the use of these commands or disable them to prevent potential abuse.

```
SEND @node SHOW USERS
SEND @node CPQUERY NAMES
```

2.2.3　*QUERY SYSTEM*

QUERY SYSTEM (Figure 2.3) is used to determine what other nodes are directly connected to a particular node. Additional line usage totals may be obtained from VAX/VMS systems with **QUERY SYSTEM SUM.**

```
SEND @node QUERY SYSTEM
SEND @node QUERY SYSTEM SUM
```

These commands are most useful for someone attempting to track down a problem with a particular line or node, but they also present interesting information for anyone wondering how BITNET works.

Chapter 3

File Transfers

BITNET allows files[1] to be transferred between people on different nodes. Sending a file is very similar to sending a message; in addition to the account name and node name for the person you are sending the file to, you need to know the name of the file you wish to send.

When transferring files, some care must be given as to the type, or class, of file. Some software used with BITNET automatically removes certain control characters from files, such as unprintable formatting characters used by editors. Also, lines that are longer than eighty characters may get wrapped, or divided into smaller lines. Only the sender may override these features, so care must be exercised in sending files.

Although there are no technical limits on the sizes of files that may be sent using BITNET, CREN rules require that files larger than 300,000 characters (300 kilobytes or 600 VMS blocks) be divided into smaller parts. Small files transfer faster over BITNET and do not create as much network congestion. Some BITNET sites monitor file sizes and refuse to transmit files that are too large. It is also recommended that

---

1. A *file* is a collection of data, often text created using an editor. Each file is assigned a file name, or tag, to identify the contents. It is analogous to a file cabinet; each folder (file) has a label (file name) identifying its contents.

```
$ SEND/FILE
_File: CYBERSPACE.CONFERENCE
_To: SMITH@SWTEXAS
```

Figure 3.1 Simple Form for Sending a File

filesthat are divided into smaller parts be sent at a nonpeak time (such as late at night), or be sent over a longer period of time (such as one part per day). Some BITNET utility programs (described at the end of this chapter) allow files to be compressed, broken into parts, and sent at set intervals.

To make file transfers easier, some nodes have implemented automated file servers for allowing access to files stored at their sites. Information on these file servers, typically called **LISTSERV** or **VMSSERV**, is included in Chapter 5, Servers.

3.1 SEND/FILE

The **SEND/FILE**[2] command is used for transferring files. The simplest form of the command is:

```
SEND/FILE
```

This command allows prompting for needed information: the name of the file to send, the user name, and the node name of the person to receive it. Figure 3.1 shows an example.

SEND/FILE is typically used with the file name and user name specified:

```
SEND/FILE filename.filetype user@node[3]
```

The file names and file type must each be eight characters or less to transfer via BITNET. Otherwise, the file name is truncated on the receiving end. The VMS operating system, however, allows file names and file types of up to 32 characters each. To compensate for this

---

2. For IBM VM/CMS systems, the **SENDFILE** command is used.

3. IBM VM/CMS systems use a space to separate the file name from the file type and the word "AT" in place of the @.

difference, the **/VMSDUMP** parameter (described later) may be used, but only when sending files between VAX/VMS computers.

When more than one file is being sent, file names may be separated by commas, or wildcard characters may be used:

```
SEND/FILE filename1.filetype, filename2.filetype user@node
```

For example, if three files were to be sent, the files could be listed together, such as *FILE1.TXT*, *FILE2.TXT*, and *FILE3.TXT*. The VMS operating system uses a percent sign (%) as a wildcard character for matching one character and an asterisk (*) as a wildcard character for matching many characters. *FILE%.TXT* specifies all files that start with *FILE*, have one more character (or none) in the file name, and have a *.TXT* file type. In addition to matching *FILE1.TXT* and the other two files mentioned, this specification would also match *FILE.TXT*, *FILEA.TXT* and *FILES.TXT* if they existed. *FILE*.TXT* specifies all files that start with *FILE*, have 0–28 other characters in the file name, and a *.TXT* file type. *FILE.TXT*, *FILE0001.TXT*, and *FILEANY-THING.TXT* all match this specification.

IBM RSCS/NJE protocols allow for four types, or classes, of BITNET files: **PUNCH**, **PRINTER**, **NETDATA**, and **BINARY**. On VMS/Jnet systems, **VMSDUMP** format files are also allowed. **PUNCH** files are a holdover from the days when punched cards were used with computers. Lines are limited to 80 characters, with longer records wrapped to the next line, control codes removed, and each line starting with a length count. **PRINTER** is used for files with lines of 132 characters or less, suitable for printing on a line printer; printer control codes are supported with this format. **NETDATA** allows files with longer record lengths to be sent; **NETDATA** is a special format typically recognized by IBM mainframes only. **BINARY** allows files to be sent "as is," without lines being wrapped or most control codes stripped out. **VMSDUMP** is similar to **BINARY** but is used when sending between VMS/Jnet systems; it pre-serves file attributes and does not truncate long file names.

PUNCH is the default file type when transferring files using BITNET. If another format is desired, it should be specified when a file is sent. This

```
$ SEND/FILE NETSERV.NAMES NETSERV@BITNIC
(SWTNYSSA) - Sent file 8127 on link UTGATE to BITNIC NETSERV
(UTGATE) - Sent file 8127 on link UHOU to BITNIC NETSERV
(UHOU) - Sent file 8127 on link RICEVM1 to BITNIC NETSERV
(RICEVM1) - SENT FILE 6933 (8127) ON LINK PUNFSV2 TO BITNIC(NETSERV)
(PUNFSV2) - Sent file 4086 (8127) on link CUNYVMV2 to BITNIC(NETSERV)
(BITNIC) - FILE (8127) SPOOLED TO NETSERV — ORG SWTEXAS(MME4FF16)  1/01/90  4:15:19 EST
(CUNYVMV2) - DMTNTR147I SENT FILE 7878 (8127) ON LINK BITNIC TO BITNIC(NETSERV)
```

Figure 3.2 Messages Returned as a File Is Sent

is done by adding a parameter to the **SEND/FILE** command, such as **SEND/FILE/VMSDUMP** to use **VMSDUMP** format.

In all, there are more than twenty different parameters that may be specified when sending files. These parameters are usually not needed. They become important when a file is not of a standard format and needs some type of conversion to transfer properly.

Parameters are included by appending a slash (/) and the parameter name onto the command name, as with **/FILE** being added to **SEND**, in **SEND/FILE**.[4] Figure 3.2 shows a sample session using **SEND/FILE**.

3.2 *RECEIVE*

If you're logged on when a file arrives for you, a message is displayed on your terminal giving the name of the file and the sender. If you are not logged on when a file arrives, a message lets you know how many new files are waiting for you the next time you do log on. Files transferred using BITNET are temporarily stored in a system directory until they can be received using the **RECEIVE** command. **RECEIVE** copies a file from the system directory into the directory you're currently using, translating it into the proper format at the same time. A simple form of the **RECEIVE** command allows all waiting files to be received:

```
RECEIVE *
```

---

4. On IBM VM/CMS systems, parameters are included by appending a left parenthesis to the end of the command line, then listing parameters after it. An IBM VM/CMS command line would have this syntax for the **SENDFILE** command: **SENDFILE filename filetype user AT node (parameters.**

```
$ RECEIVE
Files received for SMITH
Source file      Class   Node    User    Date      Time    Records
VMSSERV.INFO;3   PUN A   SWTEXAS JONES   4-Nov-89 18:16   96
USING.SERVERS;2  PUN A   SWTEXAS JONES   4-Nov-89 18:16   1066
USEGUIDE.INFO2;1 PUN A   SWTEXAS JONES   4-Nov-89 18:16   59

RECEIVE> RECEIVE VMSSERV.INFO, USING.SERVERS
%RECEIVE-S-COPIED, Copied punch file
from: VMSSERV.INFO;3
to: SYS$SCRATCHPAD:[SMITH]VMSSERV.INFO;1
%RECEIVE-S-COPIED, Copied punch file
from: USING.SERVERS;2
to: SYS$SCRATCHPAD:[SMITH]USING.SERVERS;1
RECEIVE>
```

Figure 3.3 Using RECEIVE to Transfer Files

Some caution should be exercised in using **RECEIVE** in this manner; existing files of the same name may accidentally be lost.

Specific files may also be received:

```
RECEIVE filename.filetype
```

Just as wildcard characters ("%" and "*" for VMS systems) may be used to send files, they may also be used to receive files. For example, **RECEIVE FILE*.TXT** copies all files starting with "FILE" and having a file type of ".TXT".

If **RECEIVE** is typed without any parameters, all files waiting to be received are displayed, and a RECEIVE> prompt is presented, indicating that the **RECEIVE** program is running.[5] Files may also be received at the RECEIVE> prompt, just as at the operating system level, by typing **RECEIVE** and the name(s) of the files to be received. Figure 3.3 shows two examples using **RECEIVE**.

---

5. The equivalent command on an IBM VM/CMS system is **RDRLIST**, which displays a similar list of files and allows receiving or disposing of them.

```
RECEIVE> DIRECTORY
Source file       Class    Node    User     Date     Time    Records
USEGUIDE.INFO2;1 PUN A     SWTEXAS JONES    4-Nov-89 18:16   59

RECEIVE> DELETE USERGUIDE.INFO2
%RECEIVE-I-DELETED, USERGUIDE.INFO2 deleted
```

Figure 3.4 RECEIVE DIRECTORY and DELETE Commands

Once files are received, they are removed from the system directory where they were temporarily stored.

When used from the RECEIVE> prompt, the **DIRECTORY** command (commonly abbreviated **DIR**) displays files waiting to be received. With the above example, if a **DIRECTORY** command were issued after the files were received, they would no longer appear:

```
RECEIVE> DIRECTORY
```

Another command, **DELETE**, allows the erasing of any unwanted files:

```
RECEIVE> DELETE USERGUIDE.INFO2
```

Figure 3.4 shows examples of using the **DIRECTORY** and **DELETE** commands.

Files may also be copied into your current directory with the **COPY** command, instead of being received. Files that are not received within a specified time period (set by your system administrator) are deleted.

Just as with **SEND**, **RECEIVE** has many parameters for manipulating files. Help is available at the RECEIVE> prompt by typing **HELP**.

3.3 *File Utilities*

Many file utilities have been developed over the years by computer programmers on various networks; then they have been distributed across BITNET via mailing lists. Your particular site may not have these utilities, or they may be hidden away in a network directory. Ask your system manager if you need access to one of these utilities and cannot find it.

```
$ DIR FILE*.*
Directory DISK$A:[SMITH]
FILE1.COB;1        FILE2.COB;1

$ VMS_SHARE FILE*.COB FILE.SHAR
VMS_SHARE V06.10 7-FEB-1989
SHARE_MAX_PART_SIZE is defined as 31 blocks (15872 bytes).
Looking at DISK$A:[SMITH]FILE1.COB;1
Looking at DISK$A:[SMITH]FILE2.COB;1
Checksumming DISK$A:[SMITH]FILE1.COB;1
Checksumming DISK$A:[SMITH]FILE2.COB;1
Packing files into SHARE file(s) DISK$A:[SMITH]FILE.SHAR
SHARE-file DISK$A:[SMITH]FILE.SHAR was written in 2 parts as follows:
DISK$A:[SMITH]FILE.SHAR_1_OF_2;1   31       9-NOV-1989       11:04:21.34
DISK$A:[SMITH]FILE.SHAR_2_OF_2;1   5        9-NOV-1989       11:04:20.64
Total of 2 files, 36 blocks.
```

Figure 3.5 Creating an Archive Using VMS_SHARE

3.3.1

VMS_SHARE

Computer networks and mail delivery systems are notorious for changing data in the files that pass through them. For example, as indicated earlier, the BITNET **SEND** command automatically strips control codes and wraps long lines unless told not to do so. Some mailers convert tabs to spaces, while others convert spaces to tabs, and not all use the same number of spaces to represent a tab. If all you're sending via a network is a text file, these problems are just a minor nuisance. But if you're sending the source code for a program, wrapped lines and misplaced tabs may cause the program not to compile properly, creating a programming nightmare.

VMS_SHARE[6] is a program for VAX/VMS systems that packages files for transmission over various networks. It converts files with unprintable characters (such as tabs and escape sequences) and long lines into plain ASCII text files with lines of 79 characters or less. It also breaks files into small parts; files longer than 16,000 characters (31 VMS blocks)

---

6. **VMS_SHARE.$PACKAGE** is available from VMSSERV@UBVMSA and other VMSSERV sites, if it is not installed on your VAX/VMS system. *See* Chapter 5, Servers, for instructions on retrieving files from VMSSERV sites.

```
$ COPY  FILE.SHAR_%_OF_2  FILE.SHAR

$ @FILE.SHAR
Creating FILE1.COB
CHECKSUM passed.
Creating FILE2.COB
CHECKSUM passed.
```

Figure 3.6 Unpacking a VMS_SHARE Archive

are split into multiple parts. When all the parts of a **VMS_SHARE**
file are combined using a text editor or the VMS **COPY** command, the
file becomes a self-extracting batch or command file. When executed,
this file unpacks all the files stored in it, verifying via a checksum[7]
that the data unpacked is the same as that which was put into it.

When executing **VMS_SHARE**, files to be included are listed first. The
name of the share file to create is listed last. Wildcards (the "%" and
"*" characters, described with the **SEND/FILE** command) are also allowed for file names.

```
VMS_SHARE filename1.filetype[, filename2.filetype] shar_filename.filetype
```

The share file created will have the file type specified, plus a further
file type of n_OF_m, where n is the file number, and m is the total
number of files created.

Figure 3.5 gives an example of a **VMS_SHARE** archive being created.
Since the files being put into the archive total more than 16,000 but less
than 32,000 characters, two **VMS_SHARE** files are created.

Figure 3.6 shows the same files being copied (using a wildcard) and then
unpacked into their original forms.

---

7. A checksum is a calculated number used to verify file integrity; before a file is
added to a **VMS_SHARE** archive, a checksum is calculated based on the data in
the file; it is then stored in the archive. When a file is unpacked from the archive,
the checksum is calculated on the unpacked file and compared to the original. If
they are not the same, the unpacked file did not get transferred properly. If they
are the same, the unpacked file is PROBABLY the same.

The first version of **VMS_SHARE** was written by Michael Bednarek at Melbourne University, Australia, and called **_VMS_SHAR_**. The current version is a rewrite of the original, with substantial improvements, done by James Gray of Inglewood, California. Further enhancements were made by Andy Harper at Kings College, London.

3.3.2   _LPUNCH_

LPUNCH is a VAX/VMS utility for converting files in **LISTSERV PUNCH** (also called **_LPUNCH_**) format to plain text. It works by reading lines of up to 80 characters from a file, then acting on the first few characters on each line. These characters are usually two numbers (a character count and a line count) each followed by a slash or an asterisk (which marks an **LPUNCH** comment line that is not to be converted.) File listings from **LISTSERV**s (_see_ Chapter 5, Servers) are often in this format. Typical lines in such files might look like this:

```
41/1/* LISTSERV FILELIST for LISTSERV@BITNIC.
90/2/This is a sample of a line that has more than 80 characters
and thus wraps to a second line.
* This is a comment line.
```

LPUNCH would convert these lines like this:

```
LISTSERV FILELIST for LISTSERV@BITNIC.
This is a sample of a line that has more than 80 characters and
thus wraps to a second line.
```

Note that the numbers at the beginning of each line are gone and the comment line was not converted.

Assuming **LPUNCH** has been installed on your computer,[8] it may be executed with this command:

```
$ LPUNCH filename.filetype
```

The `filename.filetype` is the name of the file to convert; the converted file will have the same name, unless a second file name is specified.

---

8. _LPUNCH.COM_ is available from _VMSSERV@UBVMSA_ and other _VMSSERV_ sites, if it is not already installed on your system. _See_ Chapter 5, Servers, for instructions on retrieving files from VMSSERV sites.

LPUNCH works with only one file at a time; wildcard characters are not allowed in the file name or file type.

3.3.3   *LZCMP and LZDCM*

LZCMP is a file compression utility based on the UNIX **COMPRESS** program. **LZCMP** compresses files into a binary format using the Lempel-Ziv file compression algorithm. **LZDCM** decompresses compressed files, restoring them to their original states. The VAX/VMS version of these programs was written by Martin Minow and based on work done by numerous programmers on the UNIX **COMPRESS** program.

Compressed files take up less disk space than noncompressed files, and they can be transmitted faster than the original files when being sent between computers. For large files that are not used often, compressing them and then decompressing them when they are needed makes sense if you are short on disk space.

If **LZCMP** and **LZDCM** are not already installed, they are available from WSMR-SIMTEL20.ARMY.MIL in the PD3:[MISC.VAXVMS] directory as LZCOMPRESS.SHARE. To access files from SIMTEL20 requires using the BITFTP server, briefly described in Appendix E, Software Collections, but this process is detailed and requires familiarity with Internet **FTP** program.

If **LZCMP** and **LZDCM** are installed on your system, they are probably invoked with these commands:

```
COMPRESS filename.filetype filename.filetype_Z
DECOMPRESS filename.filetype_Z
```

Only one file at a time may be compressed or decompressed. It is standard to use **_Z** at the end of the file type for files that have been archived using **COMPRESS**. The program itself does not add the **_Z** character.

Parameters for **COMPRESS** and **DECOMPRESS** are indicated with a dash (-), rather than with a slash (/) as with most VAX/VMS programs. One

```
$ COMPRESS FILE1.COB, FILE2.COB_Z
FILE1.COB: 57.18% compression

$ DIR/SIZE FILE*.COB*
Directory DISK$A:[SMITH]
FILE1.COB;2                21
FILE1.COB_Z;2              9
```

Figure 3.7 Compressing Files with LZCMP

parameter, **-v**, gives a verbose listing of what is being done to a file. It is used with this syntax:

```
COMPRESS -v filename.filetype filename.filetype_Z
DECOMPRESS -v filename.filetype_Z
```

Figure 3.7 shows how files may be compressed to save space and the output from the **-v** parameter.

Chapter 4

Electronic Mail

Electronic mail (commonly called *e-mail*) is simply a way to send a note on a computer to another person or to many people. Sending e-mail is similar to typing and mailing a letter via the post office (snail-mail), only much easier and faster since you don't have to physically go to the post office. Most short notes arrive within a few minutes of being sent; heavy network traffic or off-line nodes may cause notes occasionally to be delayed, but BITNET e-mail usually makes it to any BITNET destination without problems. E-mail that cannot be delivered is returned with the reason for nondelivery.

To send e-mail via BITNET, it is easiest to use the e-mail system installed on your computer since you're probably already familiar with it and the editor used by it. Unfortunately, the **VMSmail** program supplied by Digital Equipment Corporation on VAX computers does not directly support BITNET-style (*user@node*) addresses. Therefore, many sites use additional software to allow BITNET addresses to be accepted. How to use **VMSmail** is described later in this chapter, along with **PMDF**, the Pascal Memo Distribution Facility, which works with **VMSmail**. A completely separate mailing system, **gMail**, is also explained.

Before sending e-mail, a word of caution is in order. Although you may think of an e-mail note as private correspondence between you and one other person, this is not the case. System managers and other computer personnel have the ability to monitor the contents of notes and keep logs on who sent a message to whom at what time. On very rare occasions, mail systems have also been known to malfunction or be misused, causing your note to be sent to someone (or to a group of people) for whom it was not intended. Thus, you should be very careful that anything you send via e-mail would not cause you (or your correspondent) undue stress if it were suddenly broadcast to the entire world.

Of the many different services offered via BITNET, e-mail is certainly the most popular. One of the uses of e-mail, mail distribution lists (mailing lists, for short), allows people with a common interest to distribute e-mail to everyone in a group. BITNET has hundreds of mailing lists covering almost every imaginable topic. How to access mailing lists is covered later in this chapter; Appendix D, Mailing Lists, provides more information.

4.1 Mail Systems

Many ways exist for e-mail to be sent and received on different computers. E-mail between two people is commonly handled with a mail system such as **VMSmail**, that allows someone to send, read, forward, extract, and delete messages. Pascal Memo Distribution Facility, or **PMDF**, is an add-on product that allows **VMSmail** to use BITNET and other network addresses. **gMail** is a gateway mailer, directing messages to the proper gateway to other networks.

When dealing with messages from mailing lists, it is more efficient to have a system that keeps only one copy of a message and allows anyone to read it rather than having copies of that message sent to many people. Such *newsreader* systems are common on other networks, particularly on Usenet, where they were started. **ANU News** and **VNEWS** are similar VAX/VMS minicomputer newsreaders; **netnews** is common on UNIX systems.

A variety of electronic conferencing systems also exists. These bulletin boards typically are used for the posting of local messages but may also be used to receive messages from mailing lists. **VAX Notes** and **BULLETIN** are examples of two such systems for VAX/VMS minicomputers.

The rest of this section explains the meaning of information in mail files and then gives quick overviews of **VMSmail**, **PMDF**, and **gMail**.

4.1.1   *Mail Files*

Mail files are just text files with a special mail header added as the first few lines. The mail system on your node adds a header, similar to the following:

```
Date:      Mon,  4 Dec 89 23:52:00 EDT
From:      Joe Student <JOE@SWTEXAS>
Subject:   How do you send mail to Fred Administrator?
To:        Sue Professor <SUE@UTXVM>


Anything you would like to say goes here, preferably no more
than 3000 lines of text.
```

As your e-mail travels to other nodes, mail systems along the way may also add `Received:` lines to the mail header, showing that the file passed through them and was assigned an identification number for tracking.

When mail comes from a mailing list, additional information is contained in the mail header. For example, this mail might have been sent to the Discussion of Ethics in Computing (*ETHICS-L*) mailing list, which redistributed it:

```
Received: From UHUPVM1(MAILER) by UTXVM with Jnet id 1123
          for SUE@UTXVM; Mon, 20 Nov 89 10:34 CST
Received: By UHUPVM1 (Mailer X1.24) id 1118; Mon, 20 Nov 89 10:27:35 CST
Date:      Mon, 20 Nov 89 08:27:00 EST
Reply-To: Discussion of Ethics in Computing <ETHICS-L@MARIST>
Sender:    Discussion of Ethics in Computing <ETHICS-L@MARIST>
From:      "Joe Student" <JOE@SWTEXAS>
Subject:   RE: The Scents Of Academic Ethics
To:        "Sue Professor" <SUE@UTXVM>
```

Note the `Received:`, `Reply-To:`, and `Sender:` headings that were added to the message. According to the `Date:` line, the message was sent at 8:27 a.m. EST time, to *ETHICS-L@MARIST*, which redistributed it. Node *UHUPVM1* added its `Received:` stamp at 10:27 a.m. CST, and it reached its destination of *UTXVM* at 10:34 CST. *ETHICS-L@MARIST* added the `Reply-To:` and `Sender:` lines in the header so that replies to the message would go to the mailing list.

Other heading lines are also possible; a common one is the `In-Reply-To:` heading added by some mail systems when someone replies to a message. `Message-Id:` is for tracking a message; `X-To:` notes that a carbon copy of the message has been sent; `Organization:` identifies the company or organization with which the sender is affiliated. Some mail systems make use of these additional header lines, displaying them whenever message directories are requested. Some mail systems also filter out extraneous header lines by default, not displaying all the `Received:` lines.

4.1.2   *VMSmail*

VMSmail is sold with the VMS operating system on VAX/VMS minicomputers, thus making it widely used at sites with VAX computers. Unfortunately, BITNET addresses are not completely compatible with **VMSmail**, making sending e-mail between BITNET VAX sites a little awkward. To add to the confusion, many BITNET sites are also linked to a DECnet[1] network, which has node names similar to BITNET node names. This table shows the difference between two BITNET and DECnet names at Southwest Texas State University:

BITNET Node	BITNET Address	DECnet Node	DECnet Address
SWTNYSSA	user@SWTNYSSA	NYSSA	NYSSA::user
SWTTEGAN	user@SWTTEGAN	TEGAN	TEGAN::user

VMSmail only directly supports DECnet addresses; to send mail to a BITNET node without using a DECnet address, it is necessary to specify a *foreign address*. This is the BITNET address in quotes, prefixed by the name of a *mail agent* and a percent sign (%). The mail agent is a

---

1. DECnet is Digital Equipment Corporation's proprietary networking system for VAX minicomputers.

program that parses the address and sends the message. The name of the mail agent to use depends on how it is installed at your node, but two forms are common:

```
JNET%"user@node"
BITNET%"user@node"
```

To send an e-mail message via **VMSmail**, from the VMS $ prompt, type **MAIL**:

```
$MAIL
You have 3 new messages.
MAIL>
```

VMSmail presents a MAIL> prompt and notifies you of any new mail since you last used **VMSmail**. A new mail count is also displayed anytime you log on to your account.

If you receive new mail while you are logged on, a message is displayed on your screen, such as this:

```
New mail on node NYSSA from SWT::MM02885 "Mr. Mike (Michael A. Moore,
Southwest Texas State)" (10:23:10)
```

The **DIRECTORY** command displays a listing of any notes that are waiting to be read:

```
MAIL> DIR
# From                     Date            Subject
1 THENIC::SAM              11-JUL-1990     RE: Wow! I didn't think there...
2 MIL%"WHJuan@DOCKMA       11-JUL-1990     Social Security Number
3 SWT::RS01                11-JUL-1990     Info.
MAIL>
```

If there is no new mail, **DIRECTORY** shows information about old e-mail in the same directory format.

Notes are read one at a time by pressing the enter key, by typing **READ** (for the next message), or by typing the number of the note to read. Each note is displayed on the screen one page at a time.

A note may be sent from **VMSmail** with the **SEND** command, or a previously received note may be replied to with **REPLY**. Both of these commands invoke either a simple line editor or EDT (depending on your operating system version) that allows the note text to be typed in: [2]

```
MAIL>  SEND
To:    MM02885
Subj:  E-mail Test
[EOB]
*CHANGE
Your note text is typed here. The EDT editor has a command mode prompt
of an asterisk (*). Typing the word CHANGE at the * prompt allows full
screen editing of text. Pressing ^Z (hold down the control key, then
press the letter "Z" one time) returns to the EDT command line, from
which EXIT (save and exit) or QUIT (don't save and exit) may be
typed.^Z
[EOB]
*EXIT
MAIL>
```

Once a note is typed in, saving the note and exiting from the editor causes the note to be sent. Quitting from the editor without saving cancels the note with this response from **VMSmail**:

```
%MAIL-E-SENDABORT, no message sent
```

VMSmail also supports the use of the popular **TPU** and **LSE** editors or the VAX/VMS editor of your choice. The **SET EDITOR** command determines your default editor; you can experiment using different editors by setting one, then sending e-mail to yourself:

```
MAIL>  SET EDITOR EDT
MAIL>  SET EDITOR TPU
MAIL>  SET EDITOR LSE
MAIL>  SET NO EDITOR
```

When sending a note, more than one recipient may be specified by listing more than one user name in the **To:** address; separate each name by a comma. To send to a group of people on a regular basis, a

---

2. It is recommended that you always use an editor within **VMSmail**. If your system is not configured to automatically invoke one for you, use **MAIL/EDIT** to invoke **VMSmail**, or **SEND/EDIT** or **REPLY/EDIT** when sending e-mail.

distribution list, or list of the addresses of people to whom you want to send e-mail, is typically used. To create a distribution list, put the addresses of people you want to send the same e-mail note to in a file with a .DIS file type. Each address goes on a separate line, with an exclamation mark used after an address to add a comment. For example, a TEST.DIS file like this may be created at the VMS $ prompt:

```
CREATE TEST.DIS
BITNET%"XY01234"  ! Mike Jones
BITNET%"ABC1"  ! Ron Smith
^Z
```

A distribution file is used in response to the **VMSmail To:** prompt, preceded by an at (@) sign:

```
To: @distribution_filename
```

With the TEST.DIS used in the previous example, this would be:

```
To: @TEST
```

So far, examples have shown **VMSmail** being used interactively. E-mail may also be sent via the VAX/VMS command line, which is useful when you have a file to send that does not need to be edited. The simple syntax for doing this, from the $ prompt, is:

```
MAIL/SUBJECT="subject" filename.filetype
To: BITNET%"user@node"
```

VMSmail prompts you for the name of the recipient; `filename.filetype` refers to a VAX/VMS file containing only text. Executable files and other files with control characters in them will cause problems for the recipient, if sent. Sending a file from the command line is useful at times, but most people prefer using **VMSmail** interactively.

A complete listing of **VMSmail** commands is available by typing `HELP` at the `MAIL>` prompt. These are some of the more useful commands:

```
SHOW ALL          Show information about how VMSmail is configured.
BACK              Read the previous note.
NEXT              Read the next note.
EXTRACT filename  Save a note to a VAX/VMS text file.
MOVE folder       Move a note to a different folder.
```

```
SELECT folder        Select a different folder for reading notes.
SET PERSONAL_NAME    To include a header that lists your real name, net-
                     work address, or other information when sending mail.
DELETE               Move a note to the WASTEBASKET folder to
                     await erasing.
PURGE                Erase deleted notes.
```

Folder refers to a file folder, similar to a folder in a file cabinet. By default, **VMSmail** keeps three folders for you: MAIL, NEWMAIL, and WASTEBASKET. New mail is kept in the NEWMAIL folder until it is read, at which time it is moved to the MAIL folder unless you move it elsewhere. Deleted notes are kept in the WASTEBASKET folder until a **PURGE** command is issued to erase them completely. Occasionally, the **COMPRESS** command is needed given to reclaim the space used by deleted notes.

4.1.3   *gMail*

gMail is a VAX/VMS utility for sending e-mail messages to foreign (i.e. nonBITNET) addresses via Jnet and **VMSmail**. Addresses are specified as they would be on the network the e-mail is being sent to. Then **gMail** automatically adds the proper gateway address, if it is needed, and sends the message. There are no facilities for receiving mail via **gMail**; **VMSmail** handles this.

gMail was developed at the SLAC (Stanford Linear Accelerator Center) in 1986 by Ed Miller, a high energy physicist, as a replacement for the VMS version of **SENDGATE**, another gateway mailer. Although **gMail** does not require special privileges to install, it uses large routing tables and many logical names, making it unwieldy for anyone except a systems programmer or systems manager to install. If your site does not have a copy of **gMail**, it is available free of charge from Ed Miller, *GMAIL@SLACTPC*. Regular updates provide new routing tables to make sure gateway addresses are current.

gMail works similarly to **VMSmail** for sending mail, as Figure 4.1 shows. The only real difference is that **gMail** converts any address entered to a **VMSmail** or BITNET address, including a gateway name if needed, and then displays that address. By default, a copy of any message sent with

```
$ GMAIL
gMail> SEND
gTo:     SALLY@SWTTEGAN
%gMAIL-I-ADDR, gMail address: 'BITNET%"SALLY@SWTTEGAN"'
%gMAIL-I-ADDR, VMSMail address:  'MME4FF16'
gSubj:   Testing
gEnter your message below.  Press CTRL/Z when complete or CTRL/C to quit.
This is the body of the message.
^Z
%gMAIL-I-VMSMAIL, sending to all VMS MAIL addresses (conditionally)
%gMAIL-I-SEND, sending via gateway BITNET to 'SALLY@SWTTEGAN'
(SWTNYSSA) - Sent file 1991 on link SWTTEGAN to SWTTEGAN SALLY
gMail> EXIT
```

Figure 4.1 Using gMail to Send a Note

gMail is also sent to your **VMSmail** address. Online help is available by typing HELP at the gMail> prompt. Logical names and mail distribution lists are supported with **gMail**, as they are with **VMSmail**.

4.1.4   *PMDF*

PMDF, the Pascal Memo Distribution Facility, is a gateway mailer, but it differs from **gMail** in that it works from inside **VMSmail**. A patch to **VMSmail** allows *user@node* addresses, although not all sites that use **PMDF** install this patch. Those that do not must use foreign addresses, of the form *IN%"user@node.BITNET"* for BITNET e-mail and *IN%"user@node.domain"* for Internet e-mail. (Other computer networks and how to send e-mail to them are described in Chapter 6, Gateways.)

PMDF was a joint effort of a number of people at different sites:

John Carosso, Harvey Mudd College

Kevin Carosso, Space and Communications Group, Hughes Aircraft

Ned Freed, Department of Mathematics, Oklahoma State University

Mark Vasoll, Department of Computer and Information Sciences, Oklahoma State University

Ira Winston, Department of Computer and Information Science, University of Pennsylvania

PMDF requires installation by qualified computer personnel at your site. It is not available for downloading but may be ordered from:

> Innosoft International, Inc.
> 250 West First Street, Suite 240
> Claremont, CA 91711
> (714) 624-7907 (voice)
> (714) 621-5319 (FAX)

For more information on **PMDF**, e-mail may be sent to *INNOSOFT @YMIR*.

4.2 Mailing Lists

The most widespread use of BITNET is through mailing lists, which distribute messages to groups of people interested in the same topic. As the name suggests, mailing lists are simply lists of people's network addresses and names. E-mail programs allow messages to be forwarded to all people signed on to a particular list.

Mailing lists come in a variety of types; most are *public*, available to subscription by anyone, while others are *private*, requiring members to meet some requirement for joining. Some lists are *open*, allowing nonmembers to send a message to the list; other lists are *closed*, accepting messages only from members. Each mailing list has a *list-owner* or *list-editor* who is responsible for maintaining the list and any *archives*, or back issues, if any are available. The list-owner may also be a *moderator*, determining the content of the mailing list and rejecting inappropriate messages.

4.2.1 Forums, Digests, and Electronic Magazines

Three general forms of mailing lists exist: forums, digests, and electronic magazines. *Forums* are places for people to post messages on the topic at hand. They are generally unmoderated and open; anyone may send a message and it will automatically be rebroadcast to everyone subscribing to that list, regardless of content. This is the most common type of mailing list, and the simplest to administer because it is fully automated.

Digests are collections of mail messages combined in a single file and distributed, either on a regular basis or after a certain amount of mail has accumulated. Digests are typically moderated, with the moderator deciding which messages will be accepted or rejected. Many moderators reject messages that are irrelevant, frivolous, slanderous, or in violation of the rules of a particular list. Moderators may also group similar messages together, making reading a digest easier than reading the random messages for a forum. The disadvantage to digests is that they are not as timely as forums; with a forum, replies to a message may start arriving within minutes of the message being sent. With a digest, you must wait for your message to be included in the next digest, then wait for replies in a future digest. Because of this weakness, some mailing lists are organized as both forums and digests. All messages are distributed to the forum immediately, and they are also collected for a digest to be sent later.

Electronic magazines are similar to paper magazines, except they are transmitted electronically and cost nothing for a subscription. They are also similar to digests, although they are published less frequently (weekly, monthly, quarterly, or at the whim of the editor), contain longer articles, and have regular columns.

Forums, digests, and electronic magazines all have their places in BITNET. Forums are good for quick responses to questions, but they contain much irrelevant material. People writing to forums often send quick, emotional replies, called *flames*, without thinking first, particularly on controversial topics. This practice often makes other people angry; they send similar replies, prompting *flame wars* that produce a lot of mail. Digests solve these problems, but it is hard to get a fast reply using a digest. Furthermore, digests take much more work by a moderator to produce. With a digest, it's easier to follow discussions, although harder to extract a particular message for saving and retrieving later. Electronic magazines are the most conservative of the BITNET mailing lists, providing an inexpensive way to distribute serious writing. They provide much of the functionality of their paper counterparts but lack graphics, photographs, and advertising.

Network etiquette has evolved to ease the friction between computer users who never see each other face to face but may communicate with each other on a daily basis. Much etiquette has to do with posting messages to mailing lists; with an unmoderated list there are few or no posted rules to guide people. These rules of etiquette have been developed over the years:

1. *Namecalling and profanity are not welcome.* Your eloquence and logic should be enough to convince people of your point of view; if not, perhaps your viewpoint needs to be reconsidered.
2. *Be brief.* Longer posts are not as likely to be read as shorter posts.
3. *A spelling checker improves your argument.* The most reasonable post is not as convincing if there are misspellings. (If you feel the need to correct someone's spelling, do so directly rather than sending a message to the entire mailing list.)
4. *Check your facts.* There may be thousands of people reading what you post; it is much less embarrassing to post correctly the first time rather than having to make a correction later.
5. *Descriptive titles and subject lines improve your chances of getting a reply.* Some mailing lists generate more than 100 responses per day; being able to find a post by its title makes it more likely to be read and get replies.
6. *Post to the proper list.* If you're having a problem with a word processor on a PC, asking how to solve your problem on a list devoted to discussion of mainframe computers won't win you any friends. It also would not generate nearly the number of responses it would if posted on a PC list.
7. *When replying to a post, check to see if someone else has already said what you want to say.* Supporting opinions are good, but only if they introduce a new idea or make another point.
8. *When replying to a post, refresh people's memories by including part of the post to which you are replying.* Don't include the entire post; a summary of the key points or the point to which you are replying is enough.
9. *Some posts are better off being replied to directly rather than being sent to the entire network.* If a message specifically requests that replies be sent directly to them, do so, rather than posting to

the list. If you are asking for opinions about a specific product, so many people are likely to have the same opinion that it is easier for one person to summarize the replies than to force everyone to wade through them all.

10. *Always check the reply address before replying.* Your e-mail may be sent somewhere you never intended. To save yourself much embarrassment, make sure you know where it is going before you send it.

11. *Don't SHOUT; use CAPS only for emphasis.* A message typed in all caps is hard to read; if your terminal or computer can only type in caps, run your message through a conversion program before sending it.

12. *Include your name and network address at the end of your post.* Even though mail systems automatically include your return address, they have been known to get scrambled when e-mail travels across networks. Many people also have accounts with access to more than one computer network; including an alternate e-mail address increases the likelihood of getting a reply.

13. *Long message signatures annoy many people.* A message signature is used primarily to identify you. Cute signatures taking up more than two or three lines, created by making drawings out of letters or by surrounding your name in asterisks, become tired looking after they're seen for the third time. A signature longer than a message is excessive!

Humor, wit, irony, and sarcasm are often hard to detect in messages. Pointing them out to people, since they can't see your face or body language, might prevent people from getting angry at what you've posted. *Smiley faces* (turn your head sideways to view these) such as :-) and ;^) are often used in posts to indicate humor or to make sure people don't take you too seriously.

It is customary to give warnings when something in one of your posts might alarm people. ***FLAME ON*** and ***FLAME OFF*** are used to delimit angry tirades, and ***SPOILER*** is common when a movie ending is about to be discussed. On other networks, a simple form of encryption, *rot13*, [3]

---

3. Each letter in a message is rotated 13 characters; "a" becomes "m", "b" becomes "n", etc.

is used by some mailing lists to hide messages that people might consider offensive. Such a message requires a descriptive title line that also includes "rot13" to let people know the type of encryption.

Abbreviations are common with mailing lists; new subscribers can often guess at what they mean from the context in which they're being used. These are some of the most commonly used abbreviations for phrases:

aTdHvAaNnKcSe	Thanks in Advance
BTW	By The Way
IMHO	In My Humble Opinion
MOTSS	Members Of The Same Sex
MOTOS	Members Of The Opposite Sex
RTFM	Read the @!# Manual
WRT	With Regard To, With Respect To

Disclaimers are also necessary with some posts. If you are not the official spokesperson for the company or organization where you have a computer account, you may want to point out that your post only reflects your personal opinion, not official policy. Also, if you make a post about a specific product, you need a disclaimer revealing whether you have any monetary or other interest in the product or in a competing product.

4.2.3	### *Subscribing to a Mailing List*

Subscriptions to BITNET mailing lists are usually handled through list servers, programs set up provide access to mailing lists and to redistribute files such as archives of previous messages. (The file aspects of list servers are covered in more detail in Chapter 5, Servers.) With these lists, you send an interactive message (or e-mail) to the list server requesting a subscription. When a mailing list is distributed from an IBM mainframe, a message is sent to the username **LISTSERV** requesting a subscription to the mailing list:

```
SEND LISTSERV@node SUBSCRIBE list-name "your-real-name"
```
[4]

---

4. Remember that double quotes are required, or your name will be converted to all uppercase.

Note that subscription requests are handled by **LISTSERV** or the list moderator and should NOT be sent to the list itself! Mailing a subscription request directly to the list means it will be redistributed to hundreds or thousands of people who read the list, and they will all be irritated at you for wasting their time. Remember, notes about a particular topic go to the list; requests for a subscription go to the list server.

Also, many people prefer that subscriptions to mailing lists be handled via **VMSmail** rather than with the **SEND** command. While an interactive message is easier and quicker to send, there are three reasons for using e-mail instead:

1. E-mail gets forwarded if a node along the way is down—an interactive message might be lost.
2. E-mail must be used when subscribing to a list on another computer network.
3. If your VAX computers are members of a VAXcluster, **VMSmail** will use the VAXcluster name for your return address rather than a single node name, thus making signing off the mailing list easier.

In addition to subscribing to mailing lists, it may be possible to request copies of previous mailings to the list. An information file is generally sent to new subscribers giving details on how to access the list archives, if there are any. These archives are usually stored as files, accessible using the **LISTSERV** commands for retrieving files, as described in Chapter 5, Servers. It may also be possible to search the archives using database commands, also described in Chapter 5.

To sign off or unsubscribe from a mailing list, a **SIGNOFF** message must be sent:

```
SEND LISTSERV@node SIGNOFF list-name
```

If you used **SEND** to subscribe to a list, you need to use **SEND** to sign off. The message must also be sent from the same node to which you signed on. If **VMSmail** is used to subscribe, it should be used to sign off.

Finding Mailing Lists

As might be expected, mailing lists come and go with frequency. A list
of popular BITNET mailing lists is included in Appendix D, Mailing
Lists, along with information on how to subscribe to each list. It is also
possible to subscribe to mailing lists on other networks. Some of the lists
from other networks are already redistributed by BITNET list servers.
Going through a list server is the preferred method of subscribing
since it cuts down on network traffic. Chapter 6, Gateways to Other Networks, explains how to access other computer networks from BITNET.

Each **LISTSERV** node maintains a list of known mailing lists; this list
may be retrieved from the closest **LISTSERV** by using the **LIST GLOBAL**
command:

```
SEND LISTSERV@node LIST GLOBAL
```


Controlling Subscriptions

The **LISTSERV SET** command has several options for controlling notes
to/from a mailing list. **SET NOMAIL** disables any e-mail messages coming
from the list, but it keeps you subscribed to access archives. **SET NOFILES**
prevents nonmail files, such as sample programs, from being sent. **SET
ACK**, **SET NOACK**, and **SET MSGACK** determine the level of acknowledge-
ment you receive when submitting e-mail to the list; **MSGACK** means
that you'll receive only interactive acknowledgements, while **ACK** and
NOACK turn on and off e-mail acknowledgements. The default options
are **MAIL**, **FILES**, and **ACK**.

Mail Gateways to Other Networks

Sending e-mail from a BITNET site to someone on another computer
network can be a frustrating experience. Unless that person successfully replies to your note, you have no way of knowing whether your
e-mail has reached its destination. Unfortunately, even if your e-mail
reaches the person to whom you are sending it, she/he may be unable
to get e-mail back to you via the same path you used.

Other computer networks and how to send e-mail to them are described in Chapter 6, Gateways to Other Networks.

Chapter 5

Servers

BITNET servers are programs that provide automatic responses to commands sent to them. Only certain key words are recognized as commands, with the type of response depending on the command sent and the type of server. *Mailing list servers,* often shortened to *list servers,* control the subscribing to (and signing off from) mailing lists; their use was described in Chapter 4, Electronic Mail. *File servers* handle the storing and retrieving of files. *Database servers* search files (databases) to retrieve information from them. *User directory servers* provide name and address searching, much like receiving a phone number from a directory assistance operator. *Relay servers* control the sending and receiving of interactive messages between groups of people. Other customized servers also exist; for example, there is a poetry server that sends a poem to anyone who requests one.

The various types of servers do not all receive commands in the same way. Some servers respond to interactive messages, such as those sent with **SEND**. Other servers respond to e-mail, with a command in place of a subject line or in the body of the note, while still other servers respond to messages sent in files with the **SEND/FILE** command. Finally, there are servers that can handle all three types of messages. Generally, servers that require a special type of message are advertised that way; relay servers are a good example — they only accept commands via interactive messages.

Servers send information using a variety of methods and in a variety of formats. Most BITNET servers are capable of sending an immediate interactive message as a reply to an interactive message. Servers may also respond with e-mail notes and with files. Directory listings (files containing a list of directories and files available from the server) are typically sent in **LISTSERV PUNCH** format, with each line containing a length count and no line longer than eighty characters. Other files may be in any of the various formats discussed in Chapter 3, File Transfers.

A list of popular servers is included in Appendix E, Software Collections. The current list of servers is also available directly from BITNIC, the BITNET Information Center, with this command:

```
SEND LISTSERV@BITNIC GET BITNET SERVERS
```

5.1 Server Programs

Three server programs have gained widespread acceptance among BITNET users: **LISTSERV**, **NETSERV**, and **VMSSERV**. All have similar functions, although each does something the others do not. Where there is overlap in function, many of the commands used to access each server are the same.

5.1.1 LISTSERV

It is not possible to discuss servers without talking about **Revised LISTSERV**, a multi-purpose server that combines the functions of a mailing list server, a file server, and a database server in one program. The original **LISTSERV** was developed by Ricardo Hernandez at EDUCOM in the early 1980s as a mailing list server to provide mail distribution to people at BITNIC who had common interests. **LISTSERV** treated groups of account numbers as mail distribution lists, forwarding a copy of any mail sent to a particular account to everyone on the mailing list for that account. People subscribed to a mailing list by sending e-mail to the *list coordinator,* who added their names to the mail distribution list.

```
$ SEND LISTSERV@UTARLVM HELP
Revised LISTSERV version 1.6c — most commonly used commands
Info              <topic|?>                Get detailed information files
List              <Detail|Short|Global>    Get a description of all lists
SUBscribe         listname <full_name>     Subscribe to a list
SIGNOFF           listname                 Sign off from a list
SIGNOFF           * (NETWIDE               from all lists on all servers
REView            listname <options>       Review a list
STats             listname <options>       Review list statistics
Query             listname                 Query personal distribution options
SET               listname options         Set personal distribution options
INDex             <filelist_name>          Obtain a list of LISTSERV files
GET               filename filetype        Obtain a file from LISTSERV
REGister          full_name|OFF            Tell LISTSERV about your name
```

Figure 5.1 Using HELP to Get a Summary of Commands

Eric Thomas, a student at Ecole Supérieure d'Electricité (France) who worked nights at the Ecole Centrale de Paris, added most of the functions in the **Revised LISTSERV**[1] program in use today. Thomas's complete rewriting and modification of the original program brought about a major change; users may now subscribe to lists without the manual intervention of the list coordinator. Database and file functions were added as the program evolved.

LISTSERV is a server for IBM VM/CMS mainframes; it allows the efficient distribution of e-mail to remote nodes, sending only one copy of a mail message to a remote node, then redistributing that message rather than sending a separate message for each person at the node. **LISTSERV** also handles nonmail files, interactive messages, file transfers, and automated subscription to and cancellation from lists. Nonmail files sent from **LISTSERV** must be received with the **RECEIVE** command, described in Chapter 3, File Transfers.

Throughout this chapter, **LISTSERV** is used in examples for subscribing to mailing lists, retrieving files from servers, and searching databases. Figure 5.1 shows a summary of current **LISTSERV** commands; to get your own listing, a **HELP** command can be sent to any **LISTSERV**:

---

1. Hereafter referred to as **LISTSERV**.

Node refers to any IBM VM/CMS BITNET node that has an active **LISTSERV**. As you may recall, you can get the current list with the command:

SEND LISTSERV@BITNIC GET BITNET SERVERS

5.1.2   *NETSERV*

As the original **LISTSERV** gained popularity on BITNET in the United States, EARN developed another server with some of the same functions but with a slightly different purpose. **NETSERV** was created by Berthold Pasch at the IBM European Network Center in Germany to provide distributed network file and database services across all of BITNET, including NetNorth and EARN. While there may be a **LISTSERV** at each university connected to BITNET, there is typically only one **NETSERV** per country. (Although countries with a large number of BITNET nodes, like the United States, may have several **NETSERV**s, very small countries may actually be served by a neighboring country.) With this organization, there is only one **NETSERV** that services commands from any given node; commands sent to a different **NETSERV** may be honored, but not without a message being returned identifying the correct **NETSERV** to use in the future.

NETSERV provides two main functions: controlled distribution of files and user directory services. **NETSERV** differs from **LISTSERV** in that any file in a **NETSERV** directory listing is also available from all **NETSERV** nodes. **LISTSERV**s on different nodes usually have only a few files in common. **NETSERV** also differs from **LISTSERV** in that it is not a general purpose mailing list server,[2] although it is a user directory server.

LISTSERV and **NETSERV** share many commands, particularly for retrieving and managing files. Each also supports commands that the

---

2. **NETSERV** has **SUBSCRIBE** and **UNSUBSCRIBE** commands, but only for privileged users who have been assigned passwords by the node administrator. Rather than these commands being used for controlling mailing list subscriptions, they are used for file updates. Whenever a new version of a **NETSERV** file is available, anyone subscribing to that file automatically receives a copy.

other does not, since each has additional features. For a list of **NETSERV** commands, send the following **HELP** command to the **NETSERV** closest to you:

```
SEND NETSERV@node HELP
```

Figure 5.2 shows a map of **NETSERV** nodes. Only a small number of **NETSERV** nodes exist, since they are all that are necessary to efficiently distribute network software across BITNET. A current version of this map is available by issuing the command:

```
SEND NETSERV@node GET NETSERV NETWORK
```

You can send the command to any **NETSERV** node listed in Figure 5.2 but should use the one closest to your location.

5.1.3   *VMSSERV*

While **LISTSERV** and **NETSERV** run only on IBM mainframes, **VMSSERV** was written for VAX/VMS systems by Brian Nelson, of the University of Toledo, and James Gerland, of the State University of New York (SUNY) at Buffalo. **VMSSERV** is strictly a file server; it has no commands for subscribing to mailing lists or for querying databases.

VMSSERV supports **PUNCH** and **VMSDUMP** (for transferring binary files between VAX/VMS systems) file formats, as described in Chapter 3, File Transfers. Interactive commands (sent via **SEND**) and e-mail (but only in place of the mail text, NOT in the header subject line) are both accepted. A list of **VMSSERV** commands may be retrieved by sending a **HELP** command to any **VMSSERV** site:

```
SEND VMSSERV@node HELP
```

The **node** must be the name of a VAX/VMS system running a **VMSSERV** server. Although commands may be sent from IBM mainframes, file transfers in **VMSDUMP** format are only possible from other VAX/VMS sites. Different **VMSSERV** sites have also developed their own help files, so the help file received may vary between sites.

Commands may be sent to any **VMSSERV** site. Each location maintains its own collection of software, so files are typically not duplicated between

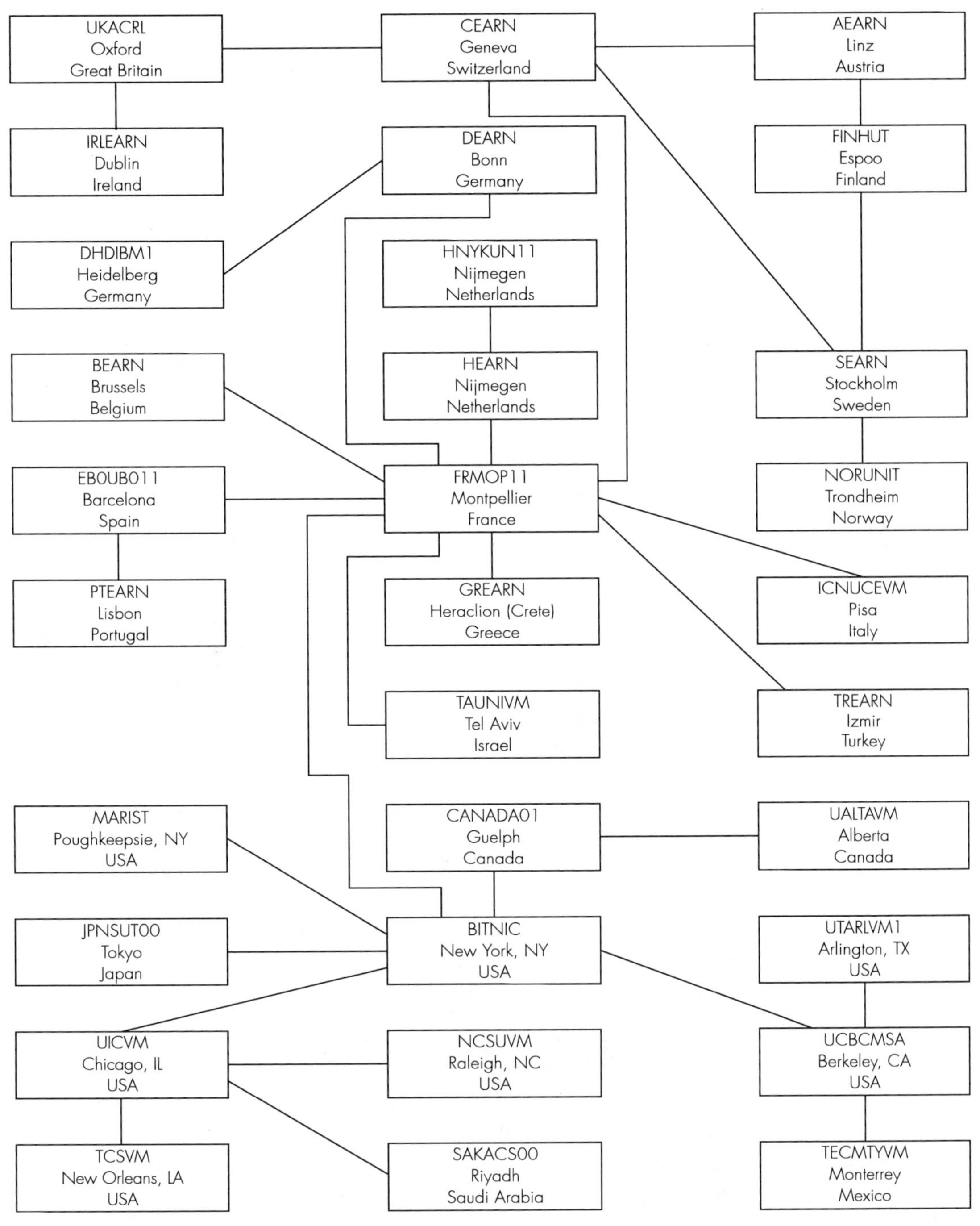

Figure 5.2 NETSERV Nodes as of January 1991

```
**************************************************************************************
*FILELIST declarations                                                              *
*Those filelists which have a PUT code of N/A are either maintained                 *
*automatically by LISTSERV or come in as part of the LISTSERV software              *
*package and can therefore not be changed by the installation.                      *
**************************************************************************************
*                          rec           last - change
*  filename  filetype  GET  PUT  -fm  lrecl nrecs date      time      File description
*  --------  --------  ---  ---  ---  ----- ----- ----      ----      ----------------
   LISTSERV  FILELIST  ALL  CTL  V    104   81    89/11/22  07:49:42  Lists all available LISTSERV files
   NOTEBOOK  FILELIST  NAD  N/A  V    95    N/A   89/09/06  07:51:47  List of available notebooks
   INFO      FILELIST  ALL  LMC  V    102   103   89/10/24  07:19:41  List of information files about LISTSERV
   TOOLS     FILELIST  ALL  LMC  V    97    162   89/10/24  07:19:58  Software tools for use with LISTSERV
   CONTROL   FILELIST  ALL  LMC  V    96    140   89/11/22  07:49:41  Control datafiles used by LISTSERV
   ACSDOC    FILELIST  ALL  VXC  V    104   38    88/12/09  09:28:44  List of SUNY/Buffalo Documentation
   CMSR5-L   FILELIST  ALL  VXC  V    104   28    89/11/20  09:57:34  List of SUNY/Buffalo CMSR5-L archives
   COAUNX-L  FILELIST  ALL  OWN  V    104   51    88/12/12  16:31:28  List of SUNY COA Unix Files
   EDUSIG-L  FILELIST  ALL  OWN  V    113   33    89/10/19  14:28:44  List of BITNET User Documentation
   GEODESIC  FILELIST  ALL  GEO  V    80    23    89/11/19  19:44:01  List of GEODESIC information files
   RFC       FILELIST  ALL  VXC  V    113   33    88/06/01  11:29:00  List of Request For Comments
   RUSTEX-L  FILELIST  ALL  RTX  V    109   97    89/10/31  13:34:24  List of RUSTEX-L information files
   UNISYS    FILELIST  ALL  UNI  V    80    25    89/09/01  09:46:51  List of UNISYS information files
   VM-UTIL   FILELIST  ALL  VMU  V    119   919   89/11/20  19:26:14  List of VM-UTIL software available
   VMS       FILELIST  ALL  VXC  V    113   108   89/06/01  14:30:37  List of VAX/VMS software available
   VMSLSV-D  FILELIST  ALL  VXC  V    113   30    89/02/13  11:42:39  List of VAX/VMS File Server VMSSERV
```

Figure 5.3 Responses to SEND LISTSERV@UBVMS INDEX

sites. Appendix E, Software Collections, provides a list of known **VMSSERV** sites.

5.2 *File Servers*

File servers were developed as an addition to mailing list servers to provide access to mailing list archives and to exchange files that people discussed on mailing lists. At the bare minimum, file servers have commands for getting a directory of files and for retrieving files. Most also have a mechanism for getting online help and for sending files to the server, although the latter use often requires special privileges. Other commands are available for maintaining and updating files on the server, but they also require privileges.

Directory Listings

LISTSERV, **NETSERV**, and **VMSSERV** all use the **INDEX**[3] command to retrieve a commented listing of files available from the server. Using **LISTSERV** as an example:

```
SEND LISTSERV@node INDEX
```

This command produces a formatted listing of files for the top-level, or root, directory. Figure 5.3 shows a sample directory listing, which includes this information:

```
GET:          Who is allowed to access a particular file. Files marked
              ALL are accessible to anyone. Other common codes are:
              LCL, for local users, or people at a particular site.
              PRV, for private use, typically members of a particular
              mailing list.
              N/A, not applicable, usually files updated
              automatically by the file server software.
              OWN, for mailing list owners or moderators.
              NAD, for node administrators (the official BITNET
              contact persons at a site.)
              CTL, LISTSERV controllers, also called postmasters.
              LCB, the LISTSERV Coordination Board, made up of regional
              representatives responsible for overseeing LISTSERV.
              Other names may also be defined locally.
PUT:          The code for the person who owns the file, or put it on
              the file server.
rec-fm:       The record format.
lrecl:        The record length of the longest line in the file.
nrecs:        The number of records (lines) in the file.
last change
date & time:  The time and date this file was put on the server or
              changes were made to it.
File
description:  A short description of the file.
```

---

3. **VMSSERV** also supports the **DIR** command, more familiar to VAX/VMS users than **INDEX**. It produces a directory listing of all files available on the server, including those in subdirectories, in a format VAX/VMS users are more accustomed to seeing. However, it does not include file descriptions, only file names, extensions, dates, and privileges.

Files maintained in the root directory of a file server often have a file type of **FILELIST**. These files contain directory listings of other files on the server. The **INDEX** command, when specified without a file name, actually retrieves a file called **LISTSERV FILELIST** [4] to produce the directory listing. To retrieve a **FILELIST** for another directory, the **INDEX** command may also be used:

```
SEND LISTSERV@node INDEX filelist
```

The **GET** command, described in the next section, may also be used to retrieve these files, once their names are known.

5.2.2 *Retrieving Files*

To retrieve a file from a file server, the **GET** command (also called **SEND** or **SENDME** by some file servers) is used. Again, with **LISTSERV** as an example:

```
SEND LISTSERV@node GET filename filetype⁵
```

If the file is available and you have the proper **GET** authorization to retrieve it, the server sends an interactive message saying the file is being sent. Some servers limit the number or size of files that may be retrieved during one day. **VMSSERV**s transfer large files (100K, or 200 VAX blocks, or greater) only at nonpeak hours, typically late at night.

Due to the various formats of files, there are multiple **GET** commands for **LISTSERV** and **NETSERV**. A file may be sent in a format different from the one in which it is stored, making the file more useful to the person getting it:

```
GETND      To GET the file in Netdata format
GETDD      To GET the file in DiskDump format
GETPP      To GET the file in Punch or Print format
GETLP      To GET the file in LISTSERV-Punch format
```

---

4. Other names are **NETSERV FILELIST** or **VMSSERV.FILELIST**, depending on the file server used.

5. Note that there must be a space between the file name and the file type. This is true only for files being retrieved from IBM mainframes (**LISTSERV** and **NETSERV** sites, for example); **VMSSERV** sites separate the file name and file type with a period.

VMSSERV does not support any of the alternative **GET** commands, although it does have **PUNCH** and **VMSDUMP** commands (used in place of the **GET** command) that are somewhat similar. Typically, a person using a VAX/VMS system does not need a file in other IBM file formats.

Once a file arrives, it may be received with the **RECEIVE** command:

```
RECEIVE filename.filetype
```

A complete description of the **RECEIVE** command is covered in Chapter 4, File Transfers.

5.3   *Database Servers*

Databases are files with a fixed organization containing information that has similar characteristics. For example, the entries for a particular mailing list (with title, author, subject, date, and text *fields*) may make up one file, or database. With **LISTSERV** mailing lists, all the mailing list *archives,* or back issues, have a file type of **NOTEBOOK** and each field may be searched individually. **NETSERV** and **VMSSERV** do not support database functions.

Database servers were added to BITNET to allow not only the searching of mailing list archives but also the ability to do so without having to transfer an entire archive to a local node. Searches are conducted on the remote node, or server, and the search results are returned when requested.

Since searches require processor time on the node containing the database, only small searches are allowed. By default, **LISTSERV** allows 20 entries to be found at a time, although this limit can be increased to 100. Both batch and interactive searches are possible with **LISTSERV**, but an interactive search requires **LDBASE**, a program to run on your local node. Batch searches are possible by sending a file to the server containing **CJLI** [6] commands for the server to execute. If you are not

---

6. **CJLI** stands for Command Job Line Interface, a batch file processing language used by **LISTSERV**.

familiar with creating batch files, you will find the interactive commands easier to use, although initially getting and installing **LDBASE** requires some effort.

5.3.1 *LISTSERV Batch Files*

Conducting a search using a batch file is effective only if you know a server has the information you want or if you are unable to access a server interactively. Creating and sending multiple batch files is a tedious and time-consuming process, thus interactive searches using **LDBASE** are recommended whenever possible.

To create a batch file for running a **LISTSERV** search, having a **CJLI** "skeleton" to start with helps:

```
//  JOB  Echo=No
Database Search DD=Rules
//Rules DD   *
command 1
command 2
...
command n
/*
```

Command 1, command 2, and *command n* represent **LISTSERV** database commands, described later in this chapter. Once the appropriate commands are filled in, this file may be sent via e-mail to the appropriate **LISTSERV**, which will execute the commands. Two files are returned to you, one a mail note explaining that your search results are on the way and the other a file called **DATABASE.OUTPUT** that contains the search results. Even if nothing was found or your search did not complete, the **DATABASE.OUTPUT** file is sent to explain what went wrong.

5.3.2 *Using LDBASE*

LDBASE makes it possible to type database commands directly and have results sent interactively, rather than as files. This method is much more convenient than working with batch files. For lengthy outputs, search results may also be sent to a **DATABASE.OUTPUT** file.

Unfortunately, **LDBASE** is not installed at many sites. Appendix C, Installing LDBASE, explains how to retrieve a copy and get it up and running. The rest of this section explains how **LDBASE** is used.

LDBASE is actually a complete set of programs, written by Jan Paul Barends of the Department of Biophysics at the State University of Leiden, The Netherlands. Some of the programs included in the **LDBASE** package are special-purpose utilities, such as **TRAP** and **SEND**. **TRAP** allows messages from a server to be captured in a file so that a record of any interactive searches done with **LDBASE** may be kept. **SEND** is a utility similar to the Jnet **SEND** program for sending interactive messages, but it is customized to work with **LDBASE**. **DBS** is the actual **LDBASE** program, in an executable format.

The command files included with **LDBASE** make running the program much easier. **STARTUP** configures your computer so that **LDBASE** may be accessed from any directory by simply typing **LDBASE**, which also starts **TRAP** and **DBS**.

The first time **LDBASE** is run during a session, it should be started with these commands:

```
@STARTUP
LDB
```

It is suggested that regular users of **LDBASE** include these commands in **STARTUP.COM** in their **LOGIN.COM** file (a command file that automatically executes at login).

LDBASE prompts you for the name of a **LISTSERV** to connect to, using a Server> prompt. Once the name of a node has been entered and a connection is established, the server responds with a message giving the name of the **LISTSERV** node, the current software version, and the computer model number. A db> prompt displays, indicating that **LDBASE** is ready to accept **LISTSERV** commands or one of a limited number of **LDBASE** commands. Figure 5.4 shows the startup of an **LDBASE** session on a VAX minicomputer.

```
$ @startup
$ ldb
%DCL-S-SPAWNED, process spawned
?  short help
$  to issue dcl commands
*  for list of databases (LISTSERV 1.5n or later)
^Z to leave and/or switch listservers
Creating mailbox and subprocess...
Server> LISTSERV@utarlvm1
start? [Y] Y
db>
(UTARLVM1)LISTSERV
Welcome to LISTSERV@UTARLVM1 - Release 1.6c, backbone server.
CPU model 4341, DASD model 3380.
```

Figure 5.4 The Start of a Session Using LDBASE

Once a response is received from a server, **LDBASE** does not immediately generate another db> prompt, but it is still ready to use.

Commands for accessing databases from **LDBASE** are included in the next section. These commands also work in batch mode.

Two log files are automatically created by **LDBASE**: **DB.LOG** and **MESS.LOG**. **DB.LOG** maintains a record of your session with a server, while **MESS.LOG** traps incoming messages.

Note that **^C**[7] and **^Y** should NOT be used to quit from **LDBASE**. This causes **TRAP** to remain running as a subprocess, and messages will continue to be captured to the log files. The correct method of exiting **LDBASE** is to enter a **^Z** from the db> prompt to disconnect from a server, then to backspace to the Server> prompt and enter another **^Z** to stop **LDBASE**.

---

7. A caret (^) character is shorthand notation for pressing the control (Ctrl) key. The control key functions only when used in conjunction with another key; thus, ^C means to hold down the control key, then press the C key one time.

LISTSERV Database Commands

The most commonly used **LISTSERV** database commands allow the listing of available databases, the searching of those databases, and the retrieving of information from databases. These commands may be entered in a batch file or interactively.

To determine what databases are available on a node, the **DATABASE LIST** command may be used:

```
SEND LISTSERV@node DATABASE LIST
```

LDBASE has a shortened version of this command; typing an asterisk (*) also displays a database list. All the databases you have access to on a node are displayed. Files you are not allowed to search do not appear in the listing.

The **SEARCH** command allows the searching of a database. The simplest form of the command is to search for a text string anywhere in the database:

```
db> SEARCH text IN database
```

LISTSERV responds with how many entries were found, anywhere from zero to thousands. Note that these entries are not displayed until **LISTSERV** is told to display them by using the **INDEX** command:

```
db> INDEX
```

INDEX produces a listing of all the entries that were found. The format includes an item number, date, time, number of records, and subject line to help you determine if any of these entries are worth viewing.

To see an entry, the entry may be printed to the screen (only in interactive mode) or transferred as a file to your node:

```
db> PRINT ALL OF entry-numbers
```

More than one entry number may be listed if you want to view more than one entry. All the *matches,* or *hits,* may also be displayed at once:

```
db> PRINT ALL
```

```
$ @STARTUP
$ LDB
Server>LISTSERV@uhupvm1
Welcome to LISTSERV@UHUPVM1 - Release 1.6c, backbone server.
CPU model 3033, DASD model 3380.
DB>SEARCH cren IN pacs-l
Search started...
->Database PACS-L, 2 hits.
DB>INDEX
Item #    Date        Time    Recs    Subject
------    ----        ----    ----    -------
000364    89/08/21    09:39   113     BITNET/CSNET Merger
000671    89/10/13    15:37   33
DB>SENDBACK PRINT ALL
* File "DATABASE OUTPUT" has been sent to you in Punch format.
Received network file DATABASE.OUTPUT from LISTSERV@UHUPVM1
```

Figure 5.5 Using LDBASE to Search PACS-L

LISTSERV has a limit of displaying 100 entries from a single search, with 20 as the default value unless it is changed. These numbers are kept low to ensure that the material retrieved is actually wanted. If your search gets hundreds or thousands of hits, you need to refine your search parameters and narrow the search to material that would be more useful to you.

In interactive mode, **PRINT** sends information directly to your terminal. In batch mode, information is sent to a **DATABASE.OUTPUT** file. To instruct **LISTSERV** to send a file, the **PRINT** command must be preceded by the word **SENDBACK**, as in this example:

```
db> SENDBACK PRINT ALL
```

Figure 5.5 shows a sample search and retrieval, using the **PACS-L** database at the University of Houston, in interactive mode. Figure 5.6 shows the batch commands for the same search. All replies are sent back in a **DATABASE.OUTPUT** file.

```
//   JOB   Echo=No
Database Search DD=Rules
//Rules DD    *
SEARCH cren IN pacs-1
INDEX
PRINT ALL
/*
```

Figure 5.6 Creating an LDBASE CJLI Batch File

If a group of words is to be searched for, quotes should surround the words.[8] For example:

```
db> SEARCH 'C programming language' IN prog-1
```

Double quotes must be used for exact matches. In the above example, not only would *C programming language* be matched, but also *ABC programming language.* Single quotes occasionally produce some unusual matches.

Note that searches are usually not case specific. If no quotes are used, or just single quotes, it does not matter if you search for *text, TEXT,* or *TeXt.* With double quotes, searches are case specific; searching for *TEXT* will not give you a match on *text* or *Text.*

Three logical operators are available for narrowing a search to specific material: **AND**, **OR**, and **NOT**. Thus, to search for anything to do with *C programming* or the *C language,* this search might be used:

```
db> SEARCH 'C prog' OR 'C lang' IN prog-1
```

Parentheses may also be used to group material. Thus, refining the above example, it is possible to search for one more condition:

```
db> SEARCH ('C prog' OR 'C lang') AND 'artificial intel' IN prog-1
```

This example returns all references to C programming that also mention artificial intelligence. To search for an opposite condition, the **NOT** operator works in place of **OR** or **AND**. For example, to search for all

---

8. Technically, if more than one word is specified without quotes, an implied AND condition exists. Matches are made on entries that contain all the words, even if they are in different places in the entry or in a different order.

references to *C programming* that do not have to do with *artificial intelligence,* this command would be used:

```
db> SEARCH ('C prog' OR 'C lang') NOT 'artificial intel' IN prog-l
```

Searches may become very complex when you use logical operators. If a search condition is longer than 80 characters, a dash should be used to continue it to the next line.

Key words may be used to determine which fields in a database are to be searched. The key words used depend on the database being accessed, but for **LISTSERV** mailing list archives, with the **NOTEBOOK** file type, these key words are allowed:

```
FROM or SENDER      the address line of the mail header
SUBJECT             the subject line of the mail header
HEADER or HDR       the entire mail header
BODY or TEXT        the message itself, without the header
ALL                 the entire message
```

ALL is the default selection for searches; to override it, one of the other key words must be used. For example, to find all the messages from one person:

```
db> SEARCH * IN pacs-l where FROM = 'Joe Student'
```

Searches may also take place using date and time information. Multiple date formats are supported, such as 12 January, 12 Jan, 12-Jan-90, 90/01/12, January, 1-90, and **TODAY**. These examples show the three key date/time search phrases: **SINCE**, **FROM/TO**, and **UNTIL**:

```
db> SEARCH * IN pacs-l SINCE january 12
db> SEARCH * IN pacs-l FROM 12 jan 89 TO 12 feb 89
db> SEARCH * IN pacs-l UNTIL 89/01/12
```

Months that are spelled out may be abbreviated to any number of characters; a month such as January may be abbreviated as Janua, Jan, Ja, or J. Conflicts in month names result in the first chronological month being selected. Years are limited to two digits; when a year is omitted, the current year is assumed. Also notice that in yy-mm-dd and yy/mm/dd formats the year must come first, not last. This is not the case for mm-yy and mm/yy formats! These formats are allowed for dates:

```
TODAY
yy
mm/yy or mm-yy
yy/mm/dd or yy-mm-dd
month
dd month or dd-month
month yy or month-yy
dd month yy or dd-month-yy
```

Times may also be included with dates, but only in hours:minutes and hours:minutes:seconds formats, such as SINCE TODAY 11:00 or SINCE 12 Jan 90 11:30:00.

More information about searching databases is available in the file **LISTDB.MEMO**, available from any **LISTSERV** by sending this command:

```
SEND LISTSERV@node INFO DATABASE
```

5.4   *RELAY Servers*

RELAY is a distributed message server that allows simultaneous conversations among many people. Where **SEND** allows messages to be sent back and forth between two people (like a phone call), **RELAY** works like a CB radio, with these channels:

```
Channels 0-99      public channels, where anyone may start or join in
                   on a conversation
Channel 1          default public channel
Channels 100-999   private channels, where you must be invited to
                   join, although you may start your own private
                   conversation
Channels 1000+     private channels, accessible only to people doing
                   research and having permission to use them
```
Channels with numbers less than zero are superprivate channels accessible only to people doing research and having permission to use them.

Once you are signed on to a channel, any messages you send to **RELAY** are redistributed to other people signed on to the same channel. You receive messages sent by people on that same channel.

There are two categories of **RELAY** users:

Class 2: Public user class
Class 3: General user class

Students accessing **RELAY** are put in Class 2 by default; Class 2 users are limited to the lower channels, 0–999, and are not allowed to sign on to a channel during peak periods, typically daylight hours. Class 3 status is restricted to faculty and staff members, plus some graduate students, and may only be used for academic conferencing activities during peak hours. To be assigned Class 3 privileges, an application must be submitted to the local **RELAY** operator.

RELAY users are restricted to signing on only to the **RELAY**(s) closest to their node. A list of **RELAY** sites appears in Appendix F, RELAY Sites, although an easier method to determine which **RELAY**(s) your node is allowed to access may be obtained by sending the **/SERVERS** command to **RELAY** at the BITNET Information Center:

```
SEND RELAY@BITNIC /SERVERS
```

If you are unable to access BITNIC, the **/SERVERS** command should work when sent to any **RELAY** listed in Appendix F. The next step in preparing to access **RELAY** is to register with the nearest **RELAY** by sending this message:

```
SEND RELAY@node "/REGISTER Your Name"
```

Registering is similar to getting a CB license: you only need to do it once per **RELAY**. Quotes are necessary around the **/REGISTER** option on VAX/VMS systems so that your name may be preserved in upper and lower case, as typed. The use of **RELAY** is restricted at some universities; if you are not allowed to use **RELAY** at a node, your **/REGISTER** command will get rejected with an error message. If you successfully register, a file will be mailed to you explaining **RELAY** rules and the

```
$ SEND RELAY@TECMTYVM /LIST
(TECMTYVM)RELAY - * Relay Version 2.02 Host RELAY@TECMTYVM (Monterrey)
(TECMTYVM)RELAY - *      Channel-Users     -Topics
(TECMTYVM)RELAY - *      1          7      oat Channel Boat
(TECMTYVM)RELAY - *      2          9      Punnany
(TECMTYVM)RELAY - *      5          10     Casino Jokes
(TECMTYVM)RELAY - *      33         11     The Gay & Lesbian Channel
(TECMTYVM)RELAY - *      43         1      TAO_TE_CHING
(TECMTYVM)RELAY - *      *Private*  1      Cyberspace Wizard
(TECMTYVM)RELAY - *      *Private*  1      PLACE
(TECMTYVM)RELAY - *      *Private*  1      Inn_&_Tavern
(TECMTYVM)RELAY - *      *Private*  1      Dr. Dark's Lab
(TECMTYVM)RELAY - * There are 83 users on 39 channels (25 channels not listed).
```

Figure 5.7 Listing RELAY Channels

commands for accessing **RELAY**. It is important to read this file to make sure you do not violate any rules and lose your privilege to access **RELAY**. Specifically, you are not allowed to:

1. Disguise your identity when registering by not using your full name or by using someone else's name.
2. Use rude or obscene language.
3. Use an obscene, offensive, or extremely long nickname.
4. Sign on to **RELAY** from more than one computer account at the same time.
5. Intrude on a private channel without first obtaining an invitation from a user on that channel. (Channel scanning, or signing on one channel after the next to try to find people on private channels, is expressly forbidden.)
6. Annoy other **RELAY** users by transmitting excessive or repetitive messages, including picture files.
7. Not follow the directives of a **RELAY** Operator.
8. Be rude and discourteous to other **RELAY** users.
9. Use other people's accounts to log onto **RELAY**, without their permission.

```
$SEND RELAY@TECMTYVM /WHO 5
(TECMTYVM)RELAY - * Relay Version 2.02 Host RELAY@TECMTYVM (Monterrey)
(TECMTYVM)RELAY - * Ch              UserID@Node      Nickname          Host-id
(TECMTYVM)RELAY - * 5              ALPHA@ALASKA      (Insaaaane)       Seattle
(TECMTYVM)RELAY - * 5               ZED@CLEMSON      (Keystone)        Tennessee
(TECMTYVM)RELAY - * 5            A01010@NMSUVM1      (Shmoo)           Seattle
(TECMTYVM)RELAY - * 5            B00122@NMSUVM1      (GeneralZod)      Seattle
(TECMTYVM)RELAY - * 5              A001@CORNELLA     (Clucka)          Ithaca_NY
(TECMTYVM)RELAY - * 5             Z9999@UMRVMA       (Madness)         Urbana_IL
(TECMTYVM)RELAY - * 5          MM02885@SWTNYSSA      (Mr.Mike)         Monterrey
(TECMTYVM)RELAY - * End of /WHO list.
```

Figure 5.8 Listing RELAY Users

Once registered, it is useful to see what channels are active and who is using them. The **/LIST** command allows you to see which channels are currently in use:

```
SEND RELAY@node /LIST
```

This command displays a list of all active channels, along with the number of people using each channel and the topics for each channel. Up to three key words may be used by participants to describe current topics for a channel. Figure 5.7 shows a sample response to a **/LIST** command.

It is also possible to see who is signed on to a particular channel:

```
SEND RELAY@node /WHO channel#
```

To find out who is signed on to all the channels, the channel number may be omitted. For users on channels 100 and above, the channel number appears as "??" since these are private channels. For the superprivate channels (with numbers less than zero), people are not listed at all. If you are already signed on to a channel and want a list of other people on it, an asterisk (*) may be used in place of the channel number. Figure 5.8 shows a response to the **/WHO** command.

```
$ SEND RELAY@TECMTYVM "/SIGNON Mr.Mike 3"
(TECMTYVM)RELAY - Welcome to RELAY, Michael Moore (Mr. Mike).
(TECMTYVM)RELAY - - - - - - - - - - - - - - - - - - - - - - - - - - - - - - - - - - - - - - -
(TECMTYVM)RELAY - |                                                                  |
(TECMTYVM)RELAY - |   III   TTTTT   EEEEE   SSSS   M         M                        |
(TECMTYVM)RELAY - |    I      T       E       S     MM       MM                       |
(TECMTYVM)RELAY - |    I      T      EEE      SSS   M M     M M                       |
(TECMTYVM)RELAY - |    I      T       E         S   M   M   M                         |
(TECMTYVM)RELAY - |   III     T      EEEEE   SSSS   M         M                       |
(TECMTYVM)RELAY - |                                                                  |
(TECMTYVM)RELAY - |                      Monterrey Relay Host                        |
(TECMTYVM)RELAY - |                                                                  |
(TECMTYVM)RELAY - |     Local ops: Abuela AA0001@TECMTYVM                            |
(TECMTYVM)RELAY - |                Hunter AB1000@TRINITY                             |
(TECMTYVM)RELAY - |                May    BB0001@TECMTYVM                            |
(TECMTYVM)RELAY - |                Mike   PP838474@TECMTYVM                          |
(TECMTYVM)RELAY - |                Snoopy DA0002@TRINITY                             |
(TECMTYVM)RELAY - - - - - - - - - - - - - - - - - - - - - - - - - - - - - - - - - - - - - - -
(TECMTYVM)RELAY - *                                                                  *
(TECMTYVM)RELAY - * Yep, RELAY is now MUCH faster than before                         *
(TECMTYVM)RELAY - * since Monterrey is now a V2 Relay !!!                             *
(TECMTYVM)RELAY - *                                                                  *
(TECMTYVM)RELAY - * Be sure to do a /HELP, so you can check                          *
(TECMTYVM)RELAY - * out the new commands available.                                  *
(TECMTYVM)RELAY - *                                                                  *
(TECMTYVM)RELAY - ****************************************************
(TECMTYVM)RELAY - Your host is RELAY@TECMTYVM (Monterrey)
(TECMTYVM)RELAY - Your last signon was at 22:43:39 on 10/03/89.
(TECMTYVM)RELAY - There are 92 users on 21 relays.
```

Figure 5.9 Signing on to a RELAY Node

To access a **RELAY** channel, you sign on to that channel with a nick-name, or, in CB radio lingo, a "handle." The **/SIGNON** command is used like this:

```
SEND RELAY@node "/SIGNON nickname channel#"
```

If a nickname is not entered, your account number will be used instead. If the channel is omitted, Channel 1 is selected by default. A sign on message, or banner, is displayed each time you sign on to a channel. Figure 5.9 shows a **/SIGNON** banner from the **RELAY** at node TECMTYVM.

```
$ send relay@tamvm1
(TAMVM1)RELAY: /list
(TAMVM1)RELAY - * Relay Version 2.06 Host RELAY@TAMVM1 (Aggieland)
(TAMVM1)RELAY - *    Channel-Users-Topics
(TAMVM1)RELAY - *          1  14 Ladys & Gents unite!
(TAMVM1)RELAY - *          3   6 The Channeling Channel!
(TAMVM1)RELAY - *          8   7 Jokes and more Jokes
(TAMVM1)RELAY - *         22   8 News Topics
(TAMVM1)RELAY: /register Michael A. Moore
(TAMVM1)RELAY: /signon Mr.Mike 8
(TAMVM1)RELAY - * You are now on Channel 8. 7 other users.
(TAMVM1)RELAY - * The topic is: Jokes and more Jokes
(TAMVM1)RELAY - <ANDY> Anyone collect Murphy's laws?
(TAMVM1)RELAY - <Split> and then the string said to the bartender,
(TAMVM1)RELAY - <c-guru> i've got an old murphys poster with programmer laws.
(TAMVM1)RELAY - <Spilt> "I'm a frayed knot."
(TAMVM1)RELAY - <pout> How about oneliners?
(TAMVM1)RELAY - <ANDY> Oh, that's bad, split.
(TAMVM1)RELAY - <Barbara> Get this. I was talking to some CS nerds last night
and one said what
(TAMVM1)RELAY - <Barbara> would you call a random access memory chip made in Los Angeles?
(TAMVM1)RELAY - <ANDY> pout: Happiness is seeing your mother-in-law's picture
on a milk carton.
(TAMVM1)RELAY - <Split> Well, tell us.
(TAMVM1)RELAY - |Change| Pip (Shaun Williams SWILLI@AUSTIN) has joined this channel.
(TAMVM1)RELAY - <c-guru> One of the Murphy's on the poster: if the code and the comments
(TAMVM1)RELAY - <c-guru> disagree then both are probably wrong
(TAMVM1)RELAY - <Barbara> The Los Angeles RAMS.
(TAMVM1)RELAY - <Barbara> pout: In computer rooms no one can hear you beep.
(TAMVM1)RELAY - <Rain> The Roman Rule: the one who sez it cant be done should
never interupt
(TAMVM1)RELAY - <Rain> the one who is doing it
(TAMVM1)RELAY - <ANDY> Good one, barb.
(TAMVM1)RELAY - <Andy> Hey, pip, you know any Murphy's jokes?
(TAMVM1)RELAY - <Split> Barb. Computer geek jokes?
(TAMVM1)RELAY - <c-guru> Zymurgy's Law of System Dynamics: Once you open a can
of worms
(TAMVM1)RELAY - <c-guru> the only way to recan them is to use a larger can.
(TAMVM1)RELAY: /signoff
(TAMVM1)RELAY - |Sign off| Mr.Mike (Michael A. Moore MM02885@SWTNYSSA)
```

Figure 5.10 RELAY Messages Being Sent

Once signed on to a channel it is possible to skip the banner each time you change channels by using the **/CHANNEL** command:

```
SEND RELAY@node /CHANNEL channel#
```

Entering a number in place of `channel#` signs you on to that channel. This is the preferred method to use when changing channels; it requires less **RELAY** and BITNET overhead than signing off and signing back on. Anytime you sign on, change channels, or sign off, a message notifies other users on a channel that you've arrived or departed:

```
(TECMTYVM)RELAY - |Sign on| User MM02885@SWTNYSSA (Mr. Mike)
(TECMTYVM)RELAY - |Change| Mr. Mike (MM02885@SWTNYSSA) has left this
channel.
(TECMTYVM)RELAY - |Change| Mr. Mike (MM02885@SWTNYSSA) has joined this
channel.
(TECMTYVM)RELAY - |Sign off| User MM02885@SWTNYSSA (Mr. Mike)
```

Messages that begin with a slash (**/**) are considered commands to **RELAY** and do not appear on other people's screens. Messages that start with an asterisk (*) are comments, which also do not appear. Any other messages sent to **RELAY** are redirected to the people signed on to a particular channel. After you are signed on to a channel, messages are sent as might be expected:

```
SEND RELAY@node "message"
```

As with the regular **SEND** command, leaving the message off means being prompted for it until a blank line is entered. Figure 5.10 shows some of the interplay that goes on with students sending messages back and forth. Obviously it is possible to have more serious conversations, but evening use of **RELAY** tends to be social, with mostly students sending messages back and forth.

Before logging off your local computer, it is very important to sign off of **RELAY**, to prevent the unnecessary wasting of resources. Signing off is done with the **/SIGNOFF** command:

```
SEND RELAY@node /SIGNOFF
```

To get a quick summary of **RELAY** commands, the **/HELP** command is available:

```
$ send relay@tamnv1 /help
(TAMVM1)RELAY - * * * * * * * * * * * * * * * Relay Commands * * * * * * * * * * * * * * *
(TAMVM1)RELAY - * /BYE . . . . . . . . . . . . . . . . . . . . Signoff from Relay
(TAMVM1)RELAY - * /Channel number [,force] . . . . . . . . Change to channel [num]
(TAMVM1)RELAY - * /COntact [relaynick] . . . . . . . . . . Show Relay contact info
(TAMVM1)RELAY - * /GETOP . . . . . . . . . . . . . . . . . Try to summon a Relay operator
(TAMVM1)RELAY - * /Help. . . . . . . . . . . . . . . . . . Prints this list
(TAMVM1)RELAY - * /IGNore [nickname] . . . . . . . . . . . Ignore a user
(TAMVM1)RELAY - * /INFo. . . . . . . . . . . . . . . . . . Send RELAY INFO file
(TAMVM1)RELAY - * /Invite nick . . . . . . . . . . . . . . Invite user to your channel
(TAMVM1)RELAY - * /LCL [relaynick | @node] . . . . . . . . Show users on a given relay
(TAMVM1)RELAY - * /LINKMsg ON | OFF. . . . . . . . . . . . Turn link messages on or off
(TAMVM1)RELAY - * /LINks . . . . . . . . . . . . . . . . . Shows active relays
(TAMVM1)RELAY - * /List. . . . . . . . . . . . . . . . . . List active channels
(TAMVM1)RELAY - * /Msg nick text . . . . . . . . . . . . . Sends private message
(TAMVM1)RELAY - * /NAmes [channel] . . . . . . . . . . . . Show users with names
(TAMVM1)RELAY - * /NIck newnick. . . . . . . . . . . . . . Change your nickname
(TAMVM1)RELAY - * /OPNames . . . . . . . . . . . . . . . . Show active Operators
(TAMVM1)RELAY - * /Rates . . . . . . . . . . . . . . . . . Display message rates
(TAMVM1)RELAY - * /REGISTER full name. . . . . . . . . . . Register full name
(TAMVM1)RELAY - * /RULES . . . . . . . . . . . . . . . . . Sends the RELAY RULES file
(TAMVM1)RELAY - * /SErvers [node]. . . . . . . . . . . . . Show relays serving node
(TAMVM1)RELAY - * /SIGNOFF . . . . . . . . . . . . . . . . Signoff from Relay
(TAMVM1)RELAY - * /Signon [nick] [chan][,force][,unshift] Signon to Relay
(TAMVM1)RELAY - * /SINce . . . . . . . . . . . . . . . . . Show recently arrived users
(TAMVM1)RELAY - * /STats [FULL]. . . . . . . . . . . . . . Display Relay statistics
(TAMVM1)RELAY - * /SUmmon userid@node. . . . . . . . . . . Invite user to Relay
(TAMVM1)RELAY - * /SWho [channel]. . . . . . . . . . . . . Show nicknames
(TAMVM1)RELAY - * /TList . . . . . . . . . . . . . . . . . List channels which have a topic
(TAMVM1)RELAY - * /Topic subject . . . . . . . . . . . . . Topic for your channel
(TAMVM1)RELAY - * /UNIGNore [nickname] . . . . . . . . . . Unignore a user
(TAMVM1)RELAY - * /Users [Detailed] [Full] . . . . . . . . Show number of users
(TAMVM1)RELAY - * /Who [channel] | [*] . . . . . . . . . . Show users and nicknames
(TAMVM1)RELAY - * /WHOIs nick | user@node . . . . . . . . Identify a nickname
(TAMVM1)RELAY - * * * * * * * * * * * * * * * * End of list * * * * * * * * * * * * * * *
```

Figure 5.11 Getting Help with RELAY

```
SEND RELAY@node /HELP
```

This produces a one screen summary of all available **RELAY** commands, as shown in Figure 5.11.

Occasionally, you may want to send private messages to someone
signed on to **RELAY**. Rather than using the regular **SEND** command and
looking up someone's node and username, **/MSG** allows you to send a
message just by knowing their nickname:

```
SEND RELAY@node "/MSG nickname message"
```

Private messages display on your screen with asterisks around a
person's nickname. If you get such a message, it is being displayed only
on your screen and is meant as a personal message. You may want to
reply using **/MSG**.

5.5 User Directory Servers

User directory servers are database servers that work with files of personal information about BITNET users. A user directory server is
often used to determine a person's network address, given some information about the person. For example, suppose you know a Joan
Smith at the University of Texas. If Joan registered her name with a
user directory server, you could query the server to return information
about everyone at the University of Texas with that name. From that
information, you could probably determine if the correct Joan Smith
was listed, and if so, her network mailing address.

The term *user directory server* is not unique for this function. Some
user directory servers are called *name servers,* although this term is
obsolete and has a different meaning on other networks. The term
userdir also has another meaning, that of a directory of user-supported
software. *Electronic white pages* has gained popularity for user directory servers in the United States, where telephone book residential
listings are printed on white paper, separate from government listings
on blue paper (blue pages), and commercial listings on yellow paper
(yellow pages). *Whois servers* are also popular.

5.5.1 Adding Your Name to a NETSERV User Directory

To add your name to a user directory, you must send your personal
data to the user directory server. Since BITNET servers were first
developed on IBM mainframes, and since IBM mainframes already

had a popular NAMES program for storing personal information, some user directory servers use a shortened version of the **IBM NAMES** database format. This particular format is used by **NETSERV**:

```
:USERID.xxxxxxxx   :NODE.yyyyyyyy                   (8)
:NAME.firstname lastname                            (52)
:PHONE.phone number                                 (52)
:ADDR.institute name, city, country                 (52)
:DESCR.job title; activities; interests; etc.       (105)
```

The numbers in parentheses show the largest field sizes allowed. Entering more characters than allowed may result in your entry being rejected or in a field being truncated.

To add yourself to a **NETSERV** user directory, the **UDS ADD** command must be included in the body of a note sent to the server. A **NAMES. NOTEBOOK** file may be created with an editor, then **SEND/FILE** used to send it. It is absolutely vital that the command **UDS ADD** appear as the first line in the file or the server will reject your add request. This example shows a sample file, ready to be sent, with John Public's information filled in:

```
UDS ADD
:USERID.JPQ001     :NODE.UTXVM
:NAME.John Public
:PHONE.(123) 456-7890
:ADDR.University of Erewhon, Buckwheat, Texas, USA
:DESCR.Programmer; cave explorer; roller skater
```

With **NETSERV**, each country has only one user directory server. *NETSERV@BITNIC* fulfills this function for the entire United States. A **NAMES NOTEBOOK** file is being sent to *NETSERV@BITNIC* with this example:

```
SEND/FILE NAMES.NOTEBOOK NETSERV@BITNIC
```

If **NETSERV** finds any errors with the file, a rejection notice will be returned immediately. If there are no errors, **NETSERV** sends a message saying you were added to the user directory database.

```
$ SEND NETSERV@BITNIC UDS FIND :ADDR TEXAS
(BITNIC)NETSERV - * Message: (195) 8 entries satisfying your search criteria have been found.
(BITNIC)NETSERV - * 56: Y-P Smith (ALPHA@TAMCHEM) (409)845-0123
(BITNIC)NETSERV - * 234: Lee Jones (BETA@TAMVM1) (409)260-4567
(BITNIC)NETSERV - * 258: Y-P Smith (ALPHA@TAMCHEM) (409)845-0123
(BITNIC)NETSERV - * 129: Bruce Doe (GAMMA@UNTVAX)
(BITNIC)NETSERV - * 617: Bruce Doe (GAMMA@NTSUVAX)
(BITNIC)NETSERV - * 653: Lee Jones (DELTA1@TAMVM1) (409)845-8901
(BITNIC)NETSERV - * 856: Lee Jones (ZETA5@TAMVM1) (409)845-8901
(BITNIC)NETSERV - * 896: Judd A. Roe (JUDD@ROE) (713)668-2345
```

Figure 5.12 Searching a NETSERV User Directory with UDS FIND

5.5.2 *Searching a NETSERV User Directory*

Commands for searching a user directory are less complex than those for searching other types of databases. **NETSERV** allows two types of searches, **UDS FIND** and **UDS GET**, each of which requires a field name to be entered with the search. **UDS FIND** returns names, network addresses, and phone numbers interactively. **UDS GET** returns all information about a person, but only via mail.

Both **UDS FIND** and **UDS GET** take the same parameters:

```
SEND NETSERV@node UDS FIND search_limit :field_name search_data
SEND NETSERV@node UDS GET search_limit :field_name search_data
```

Search_limit is an optional parameter. By default, a maximum of 20 entries is returned, although this number may be increased to 100 if a value is entered. Searches are not case sensitive; lowercase or upper-case letters may be entered for the search data. Only certain key words are allowed for field names: **USERID**, **NODE**, **NAME**, **PHONE**, **ADDR**, and **DESCR**.[9] They must be preceded by a colon (:) and must be spelled correctly for successful searches.

Figures 5.12 and 5.13 show the same search using **UDS FIND** and **UDS GET**. Note that some of the names returned are duplicates; old entries are automatically replaced by new entries, but they must come from the

---

9. One other keyword is allowed: **NICK**. Instead of containing a nickname for some-one, this field contains an entry number in the **NETSERV** user directory; it is not very useful for most searches.

```
$ SEND NETSERV@BITNIC UDS GET :ADDR TEXAS
From: NETSERV at BITNIC
Command: UDS GET 30 :ADDR TEXAS
Message: (195) 8 entries satisfying your search criteria have been found.
:nick.56 :userid.ALPHA :node.TAMCHEM :name.Y-P Smith :phone.(409) 845-0123
:addr.CHEM Dept;Texas A&M Univ;College Station, TX 77843
:descr.Computer Manager
:nick.234 :userid.BETA :node.TAMVM1 :name.Lee Jones :phone.(409)260-4567
:addr.Texas A&M University
:nick.258 :userid.SYS :node.TAMCHEM :name.Y-P Smith :phone.(409) 845-0123
:addr.Chem Dept;Texas A&M Univ;College Station, TX 77843
:descr.Computer Manager
:nick.129 :userid.GAMMA :node.UNTVAX :name.Bruce Doe
:addr.University of North Texas; Denton, TX; USA
:descr.Comp Sci grad student, teaching fellow; VAX;RelayOp(nick=Hrair);AI;cats;Esalen-style
massage;psychology
:nick.617 :userid.GAMMA :node.NTSUVAX :name.Bruce Doe
:addr.University of North Texas; Denton, TX; USA
:descr.Comp Sci grad student, teaching fellow; VAX;RelayOp(nick=Hrair);AI;cats;Esalen-style
massage;psychology
:nick.653 :userid.DELTA1 :node.TAMVM1 :name.Lee Jones :phone.(409)845-8901
:addr.Texas A&M University
:descr.Computing Services Center;Academic VAX Systems
:nick.856 :userid.ZETA5 :node.TAMVM1 :name.Lee Jones :phone.(409) 845-8901
:addr.Texas A&M University
:descr.Computing Services Center;Academic VAX Systems
```

Figure 5.13 Searching a NETSERV User Directory with UDS GET

same account number and node. This policy presents a problem at universities where students change accounts each semester and node names get changed every few years. Fortunately, old data is removed from the **NETSERV** database on a regular basis. People are automatically sent a reminder once a year to update their personal data.

Multiple field names and search data may also be entered, by appending them to the end of a search line. For example, to search for someone named Joe with an address in New Jersey:

```
SEND NETSERV@BITNIC UDS GET :NAME Joe :ADDR New Jersey
```

```
$ SEND WHOIS@ALBNYVM1 HELP
(ALBNYVM1)WHOIS - * WHOIS will look up a name for you in the
(ALBNYVM1)WHOIS - * University at Albany faculty/staff
(ALBNYVM1)WHOIS - * directory.  Your query should consist
(ALBNYVM1)WHOIS - * solely of the person's last name, e.g.,
(ALBNYVM1)WHOIS - * Edwards, Le May, O'Brien, and should
(ALBNYVM1)WHOIS - * appear on the SUBJECT line or in the
(ALBNYVM1)WHOIS - * first line of the message area of your
(ALBNYVM1)WHOIS - * note or mail. Or you may specify at
(ALBNYVM1)WHOIS - * least two letters followed by an "*", in
(ALBNYVM1)WHOIS - * which case ALL names starting with the
(ALBNYVM1)WHOIS - * given letters will be reported. Aside
(ALBNYVM1)WHOIS - * from the name you specify, other
(ALBNYVM1)WHOIS - * sound-alike names in the directory will
(ALBNYVM1)WHOIS - * be suggested.

$ SEND WHOIS@ALBNYVM1 ROE
(ALBNYVM1)WHOIS - * Name: Roe, Kathleen; Phone: (518)442-0123;
(ALBNYVM1)WHOIS - *   Office: Atmospheric Sciences Rsrch Ctr; E-mail: none
(ALBNYVM1)WHOIS - * Name: Roe, Lowes L; Phone: (518)442-4567;
(ALBNYVM1)WHOIS - *   Office: Physical Education 342; E-mail: none
(ALBNYVM1)WHOIS - * Name: Roe, Mary K; Phone: (518)442-8901;
(ALBNYVM1)WHOIS - *   Office: Student Health; E-mail: none
(ALBNYVM1)WHOIS - *
(ALBNYVM1)WHOIS - * Other possibly similar names:
(ALBNYVM1)WHOIS - *   Ray, Rae, Rho, Roy
```

Figure 5.14 Searching a WHOIS User Directory

Note that spaces are allowed in strings when searching; multiple spaces are compressed into a single space.

5.5.3   *Other User Directories*

Many universities have their own user directory servers, which get updated on a monthly or semester basis. A complete list of these servers has not been compiled, although some are listed in Appendix G, User Directory Servers. *COMSERVE@RPIECE* has a popular user directory server for people located in the United States. Some networks have projects underway to unite user directory servers in a distributed fashion so that you can search for someone on multiple servers just by sending a search command to one server.

```
$ SEND BIALIK@BRANDEIS POEM
From:      Bialik Poetry Server <Bialik@Brandeis>
Subject:   Poem number 890303
           To a Romantic
      To Robert Penn Warren
Allen Tate
You hold your eager head
Too high in the air, you walk
As if the sleepy dead
Had never fallen to drowse
From the sublimest talk
Of many a vehement house.
Your head so turned turns eyes
Into the vagrant West;
Fixing an iron mood
In an Ozymandias' breast
And because your clamorous blood
Beats an impermanent rest
You think the dead arise
Westward and fabulous:
The dead are those whose lies
Were doors to a narrow house.
```

Figure 5.15 Poem from the Bialik Poetry Server

Other than **NETSERV**, few user directory servers have been set up to
work exactly the same way. Figure 5.14 shows two commands sent to a
WHOIS server at the University of Albany. Most user directory servers
do have commands to provide help on how to search them, although it
is not always possible to have your name listed on them.

5.6 Other Servers

Servers exist for a variety of purposes, although finding the exact one
you want can be a bit of a problem. A project is underway on NSFNET,
a national network of which BITNET is a member, to provide information about accessing all network resources. Resources will be classified by type, with each resource listed on a separate page that includes
instructions on how to access it. Instructions for accessing the network resources list will be made widely known when it is available
on BITNET.

```
$ SEND BIALIK@BRANDEIS INFO
From:         Bialik Poetry Server <Bialik@Brandeis>
Subject:      Poem server help file
BIALIK Poetry Server, Brandeis University   August 17, 1987
BIALIK is a BITNET server for poetry.
The three commands that BIALIK accepts are POEM, INDEX, and HELP. These commands must be sent
as interactive messages to the user BIALIK at node BRANDEIS; mail and files are not accepted.
All commands and qualifiers may be abbreviated to three letters.
***** POEM (synonyms: GET, SENDME)
Request a poem.
POEM alone, or POEM/DAY, gets you the Poem of the Day; if there is no poem for today, you get
a randomly-selected poem from the past.
POEM/RANDOM gets you a randomly-selected poem.
POEM <date> gets you a specific poem.  The number for each poem is an encoding of the date it
was slated as Poem of the Day: for example, the command POEM 870520 gets you the poem from May
20, 1987.
***** INDEX (synonym: LIST)
Request an index to all available poems.  The index displays the number, author, title, and
first line of every poem.
By adding a qualifier to the INDEX command you can select how this index is sorted: the op-
tions are /TITLES, /AUTHORS, /DATES, and /FIRST_LINES.  The default is /AUTHORS.  (You may
only use one of these qualifiers at a time.)
***** HELP (synonym: INFO)
Request a copy of this help file.
***** Other qualifiers
All three commands can take one further qualifier, which specifies how the requested file is
to be sent.  The options are /MAIL, /NETDATA, /PRINTER, /PUNCH, and /VMSDUMP.  For the HELP
and POEM commands the default is /MAIL; for the INDEX command the default is /PRINTER.  The
help and poem files contain no lines longer than 80 characters, but the lines in the index
files are up to 130 characters long and will be wrapped around if sent using /MAIL or /PUNCH.
Examples:
        POEM 870520/VMSDUMP
        POEM/PRINTER 870520
        IND/FIR/NET
***** Other
Chaim Nachman Bialik (1873-1934) is the greatest Hebrew poet of modern times.
Questions, comments, and suggestions may be sent by mail to username LAV at node BRANDEIS.
```

Figure 5.16 Information from the Bialik Poetry Server

Figures 5.15 and 5.16 show the workings of the poetry server BIALIK
at the University of Maine; it sends a poem of the day to anyone who

```
$ SEND UH-INFO@UHUPVM1 HELP
(UHUPVM1)UH-INFO - The servers available at UHUPVM1 are:
(UHUPVM1) -
(UHUPVM1)UH-INFO - PACS       ( * LIBPACS USERS * )
(UHUPVM1)UH-INFO - ATARINET   ( * Atari ST Users Group * )
(UHUPVM1)UH-INFO - EDUCATE    ( * Seminar Listings * )
(UHUPVM1)UH-INFO - INFOSERV   ( * Documentation/Publications * )
(UHUPVM1)UH-INFO - PSYCHNET   ( * Educational Psychology * )
(UHUPVM1) -
(UHUPVM1)UH-INFO - For more info on the individual server command
(UHUPVM1)UH-INFO - messages, send the message " name HELP " where
(UHUPVM1)UH-INFO - "name" is any of the servers mentioned above.
(UHUPVM1) -
(UHUPVM1)UH-INFO - In order to send a comment to UH-INFO send the
(UHUPVM1)UH-INFO - comment message preceded by an asterisk (*).


$ SEND UH-INFO@UHUPVM1 INFOSERV HELP
(UHUPVM1)UH-INFO - Valid INFOSERV Server command messages are:
(UHUPVM1)UH-INFO - INFOSERV SEND filename filetype (to obtain a file)
(UHUPVM1)UH-INFO - INFOSERV NEWS (to get the latest server news)
(UHUPVM1)UH-INFO - INFOSERV INDEX (to obtain a list of available files)
(UHUPVM1)UH-INFO - INFOSERV HELP (to display this message)


$ SEND UH-INFO@UHUPVM1 INFOSERV NEWS
(UHUPVM1)UH-INFO - +++++++++++++++++++++++++++++++++++++++++++++++++++++++++++++++
(UHUPVM1)UH-INFO - +   Welcome to INFOSERV at UHUPVM1.                    +
(UHUPVM1)UH-INFO - +   Currently available are University                +
(UHUPVM1)UH-INFO - +   of Houston, University Computing                  +
(UHUPVM1)UH-INFO - +   documents and some vendor manuals.                +
(UHUPVM1)UH-INFO - + ---------------------------------------------------------------+
(UHUPVM1)UH-INFO - +   Send any comments or questions to                 +
(UHUPVM1)UH-INFO - +   userid INFOSERV at UHUPVM1.                       +
(UHUPVM1)UH-INFO - +++++++++++++++++++++++++++++++++++++++++++++++++++++++++++++++
```

Figure 5.17 The UH-INFO Server

requests one. Figure 5.17 shows the output from UH-INFO, an information server for the University of Houston. It has guides and manuals available online explaining how to access other networks, send electronic mail, and work with various text editors. These examples show just a few of the many different resources available from BITNET servers; many more are available, but you have to look to find them.

Chapter 6

Gateways to Other Networks

John Quarterman has applied the term *The Matrix* [1] to all the connected computer networks in the world. This reference includes commercial networks, such as Compuserve and The Well, as well as BITNET, UUCP, the Internet, and thousands of others. *Gateways* [2] link many of the networks to each other for the purpose of exchanging files and electronic mail. It is now possible to send an electronic mail message from almost any node in The Matrix to any other. However, getting your e-mail correctly addressed and sent through the proper gateway(s) can be a frustrating task. Tools such as **PMDF** and **gMail** (both covered in Chapter 4, Electronic Mail) add gateway addresses to e-mail and make this task much easier—but they can help only so much. Furthermore, getting your message delivered is only half the job; the person on the other side of a gateway must address his/her e-mail properly to respond to you.

The RSCS/NJE protocols for sending and receiving messages define the addressing syntax (*user@node* or *user AT node*) used with BITNET. VNET, IBM's internal network, uses the same RSCS/NJE protocols

---

1. From William Gibson's science fiction novel, *Neuromancer.*

2. A *gateway* is a computer that is a member of two or more networks and is capable of transferring electronic mail between them.

Syntax	Example	Protocol	Network
user@node	JOE@UTADNX	RSCS/NJE	BITNET, VNET
user@node.domain	JOE@UTADNX.CC.UTEXAS.EDU	TCP/IP	the Internet, CSNET
node::user	UTADNX::JOE	DECnet	SPAN, EASYnet
node!user	ut-emx!joe	UUCP	UUCP, Usenet, UUNET

Figure 6.1 One User with Four Network Addresses

and thus uses the same syntax. Other networks, based on other protocols, use different addressing schemes, as shown in Figure 6.1.[3] For more information on other computer networks, *see* Appendix B, Recommended Reading, which includes three books that cover United States and worldwide networks. These books also include detailed maps of each network, showing major nodes and the gateways between networks.

When sending e-mail through a gateway, e-mail is sent to the gateway node (actually to an account on the gateway node), which strips off the gateway address, then resends the e-mail using the real address. Occasionally it is necessary to send e-mail to a gateway between BITNET and another network and then through another gateway to get your message to the right person on a third network.

When two or more networks are using the same protocols and there is a connection between the networks, they are considered an *internet.* BITNET, EARN, and NetNorth make up an internet. Many other networks are also internets. Some confusion may arise with the word "internet" because there is another network called the *Internet,* spelled with a capital "I."

One of the differences between BITNET and other networks lies in the use of domains. A *domain* is a grouping of like nodes capable of communicating with each other. Domains may include one computer or thousands. For example, the University of Texas has nodes that are members of the Internet *.EDU* domain, or educational institution domain, consisting of university computers around the world. At the

---

3. The term *node* is being used in these examples for consistency. *Host* is a synonym commonly used on other networks. *user@node* and *user@host* are equivalent.

same time, the University of Texas has its own domain, consisting of nodes at various University of Texas campuses, and referred to as *.UTEXAS*. Thus, Internet sites at the University of Texas are of the form *node.UTEXAS.EDU,* as in *EMX.UTEXAS.EDU*. Other domains also exist at the University of Texas, with Computer Center computers using *.CC*, as in *UTADNX.CC.UTEXAS.EDU*. When people on other networks send mail to BITNET, they typically include *.BITNET* as the domain for BITNET addresses.

<table>
<tr><td>

6.1

</td><td>

TCP/IP Networks

</td></tr>
</table>

TCP/IP (Transmission Control Protocol/Internet Protocol) are the two most well known *protocols,* or communications definitions, of the Internet Protocol Suite. (A *protocol suite* is a group of protocols that collectively define how the different parts of a computer network communicate with each other.) The Internet Protocol Suite was originally developed for ARPANET in 1980, but it was rapidly adopted by other networks connecting to ARPANET. Internet Protocol Suite networks, commonly called TCP/IP networks, are collectively referred to as the Internet.

TCP/IP networks use a *user@node.domain* syntax. Addresses often include multiple domains, as in *user@node.domain.domain.domain*. These top-level domains exist:

```
.COM        Commercial Sites
.EDU        Educational Institutions
.MIL        U.S. Military Sites
.GOV        Other U.S. Government Sites
.NET        Network Resource Centers
.ORG        Nonprofit Organizations
```

In the recent past, another top-level domain, *.ARPA,* was used to help in the conversion to domain-style names. Prior to 1980, only node names were in use, similar to current BITNET node names. In 1983, any nodes that had not converted to a domain style name automatically were grouped in the *.ARPA* domain. A more recent development in domain names has been to use two letter country codes for the top-level domain, with other domains of state abbreviations, city or site names, and building or department names. For example, the XYZ Company in Austin, Texas, might have computers in its accounting and shipping departments, with domain names of *ACCT.XYZ.AUSTIN.TX.US* and *SHIP.XYZ.AUSTIN.TX.US*. Under the old naming scheme, the computers might have be known as *ACCT.XYZ.COM* and *SHIP.XYZ.COM,* presenting naming problems if XYZ Company opened a new office in another city.

Technically, each domain of an Internet domain name may be up to 64 characters in length. Most domains are kept to 12 or fewer characters to make them easier to use. Each domain also has an associated number. Nodes were named to make them easy to remember, but these names are translated into routing numbers before they are actually used. When sending mail to a new node, it may be necessary to refer to it by routing numbers if the routing tables have not been updated for the new name.

TCP/IP networks have two features not found in BITNET: remote logins and anonymous file transfers. Through a program called **TELNET**, users at any Internet node may log on to any other Internet node where they have an account, by going through the Internet. Another program, **FTP**, or File Transfer Program, allows users to log on anonymously to other nodes for the purpose of transferring files between the computers. While BITNET has file servers such as **LISTSERV** to display directories and to automate file transfers, Internet users rely on **FTP**, which supports both text and binary file transfers.

Both **VMSmail** and **Jnet** do not recognize *user@node.domain* style names; **PMDF** does.

Whenever mail is sent through a gateway, your return address should be included somewhere in the body of your message in case a gateway or foreign mail system removes or mangles your address in the header.

6.1.1   *The Internet*

In 1969, the U.S. Department of Defense Advanced Research Projects Agency created an experimental computer network to link military bases with research sites (including universities and companies doing military research) around the world. The network was a huge success, eventually evolving to allow millions of people to communicate with each other via electronic mail on a daily basis. The network still exists today, but is officially called the Defense Data Network (DDN), with ARPANET specifically referring to the nonmilitary portion of the network (phased out in 1990), and MILNET being the unclassified military portion. Three classified military networks are also a part of DDN. Connected to DDN are many special purpose, regional, and campus networks using TCP/IP protocols; together with DDN they make up a logical network, the Internet.

DDN has a Network Information Center at Stanford Research Institute in Palo Alto, California. One node, *NIC.DDN.MIL*, is operated by Bolt, Beranek, and Newman, Inc. (BBN) specifically to provide network support services. On this node are hundreds of files describing the Internet Protocol Suite, plus a file listing all the known Internet mailing lists, **NETINFO:INTEREST-GROUPS.TXT**.

6.1.2

NSFNET

The National Science Foundation Network, NSFNET, began in 1986 as a network linking six NSF supercomputers across the United States. NSFNET now consists of a high speed backbone using multiple links connecting supercomputer sites. Independently operated and autonomous regional networks, called midlevel networks in NSFNET terminology, connect to the backbone and also provide international links. People accessing NSFNET supercomputers do so via campus networks connected to these midlevel networks. BITNET became an NSFNET midlevel network in 1989, using the NSFNET backbone to help move network traffic across the United States.

The NSFNET backbone is managed by a nonprofit consortium of eight Michigan universities, MERIT, Inc. A MERIT/NSFNET Information Services center is operated as *NIS.NSF.NET*, which also has files accessible via a BITNET file server, *NIS-INFO@MERIT*. (Send the word **HELP** in a mail message to receive instructions for accessing *NIS-INFO*.)

VAX minicomputers may be linked using DECnet, Digital Equipment Corporation's Digital Networking Architecture (DNA) networking software. Since DECnet is sold with each VAX, it is widely used at sites with more than one VAX computer. DECnet allows file transfers between nodes, remote logins, and the exchange of **VMSmail** messages.

The term *DECnet Internet* identifies a global collection of cooperatively managed, but autonomous, networks using DECnet. SPAN (the Space Physics Analysis Network), HEPnet (the High Energy Physics Network), and THEnet (the Texas Higher Education Network), are examples of large DECnet networks.

DECnet uses a *node::user* addressing syntax, although nodes are identified internally by area numbers and node numbers. Due to conflicts in area numbers at different sites, a *node::node::user* syntax has also evolved, where nodes act as gateways for accessing other DECnet nodes.

Remote file access is by VAX/VMS operating system commands; some nodes have anonymous directories set up like the Internet. They may be accessed with the VMS directory (**DIR**) and copy (**COPY**) commands by specifying only the node name, such as in **DIR node::**.

VMSmail supports DECnet addressing; messages may be addressed as:

```
To: node::user
```

Routing through multiple gateways may also work at your site:

```
To: node::node::user
```

If necessary, more nodes may be strung together to get your message to the correct node.

6.2.1 SPAN

The Space Physics Analysis Network (SPAN) was created by NASA in 1981 to connect researchers at universities with researchers and administrators at space flight centers. In its first eight years, SPAN grew to include 2600 computers around the world. The United States portion of SPAN is often identified as *US-SPAN,* and the European portion is known as *E-SPAN.*

The National Space Science Data Center (NSSDC) at Goddard Space Flight Center in Maryland provides management services for SPAN, also maintaining an online database, *NSSDCA::SPAN_NIC.* Questions about SPAN should be directed to the Network Manager, *NSSDCA::NETMGR,* also accessible from the Internet as *NETMGR@NSSDCA.GSFC.NASA.GOV.*

<table>
<tr><td>

6.2.2

</td><td>

HEPnet (ESnet)

</td></tr>
</table>

The High Energy Physics Network (HEPnet) was developed in the early 1980s by the United States Department of Energy to link its high energy physics laboratories (linear accelerator sites) with universities and other research sites. Recently other energy research disciplines, including nuclear physics and fusion, have also been included. Today, there are over 2500 computers all over the world linked via HEPnet. HEPnet is slowly evolving into the Energy Sciences Network (ESnet), which supports protocols other than DECnet.

The major routing site for HEPnet traffic is the Fermi National Accelerator Laboratory (FERMILAB) in Illinois. A network information center does not exist for HEPnet, although data about HEPnet is available from the network information centers of other networks.

<table>
<tr><td>

6.2.3

</td><td>

THEnet

</td></tr>
</table>

The Texas Higher Education Network (THEnet) was formed in 1986 to link all institutions of higher learning in Texas. With over 1200 nodes, THEnet is one of the larger regional networks in the United States.

THEnet is administered by the University of Texas System Office of Telecommunication Services in Austin. A network information center is accessible from THEnet as node *THENIC::,* or via anonymous **FTP** from the Internet, as *NIC.THE.NET.* The file *README.LIS* provides information about *THENIC* directories and files.

Some confusion exists over the usage of the terms *UUCP* and *Usenet.* UUCP is a networking facility for computers using the UNIX operating system; a *uucp* (Unix-to-Unix-CoPy) *program* is a part of UUCP and allows mail and files to be sent to remote users, and allows remote logins. Usenet (for "user's network") is the world-wide network of computers that run the UNIX operating system and the *netnews* software for exchange of network mail. Usenet is possible due to UUCP; and, as with the confusion with many protocols, Usenet is sometimes referred to as UUCP, and vice-versa.

UUCP nodes are typically connected via dial-up lines; busy sites may connect with each other at hourly intervals, while other sites may connect only once a day or less.

Since Usenet is primarily a network for distributing mail, it is not surprising that it has become famous for its discussion groups. These discussion groups, or *newsgroups,* have been divided into seven major subject categories:

```
comp       computer science

sci        science

news       netnews software and general network information

rec        recreation

soc        social interaction and society

talk       extended discussions

misc       groups that do not fit into other categories
```

Further refinements occur within each newsgroup—for example, *rec.arts.sflovers* (for science fiction readers) and *rec.games.chess* (for people who play chess). Many of the Usenet newsgroup discussions are transferred to other networks, particularly to the Internet and BITNET.

UUCP uses a *node!user* syntax, as in *ut-emx!joe.* When spoken, the exclamation point is pronounced as "bang." *ut-emx!joe* would be spoken as "u-t-dash-e-m-x-bang-joe." Unlike most other networks, uppercase and lowercase letters are significant; *ut-emx!joe* is not necessarily the same person as *ut-emx!JOE.* Although UUCP is moving toward a system with intelligent routers that recognize user@node addresses,

```
$ SEND @PSUVAX1 UUPATH 6SIGMA2
(PSUVAX1) - Path to 6sigma2:  rutgers!uw-beaver!sumax!thebes!6sigma2!username

$ SEND @PSUVAX1 UUHOSTS 6SIGMA2
(PSUVAX1) - UUCP mail path from psuvax1 to 6sigma2:
(PSUVAX1) - 6sigma2 rutgers!uw-beaver!sumax!thebes!6sigma2!%s
(PSUVAX1) -
(PSUVAX1) - UUCP mail information for host 6sigma2 (#USENET lines show USENET news links):
(PSUVAX1) - #Name                 6sigma2
(PSUVAX1) - #System-CPU-OS        Motorola VME/10; System V/68 Release 2
(PSUVAX1) - #Organization         Six Sigma CASE, Inc.
(PSUVAX1) - #Contact              Hunter Zuker
(PSUVAX1) - #Electronic-Address   6sigma2!zuker
(PSUVAX1) - #Telephone    +1 206 451 9322
(PSUVAX1) - #Postal-Address       PO Box 40316, Bellevue, WA  98004
(PSUVAX1) - #Written-by           6sigma2!zuker (Hunter Zuker);
                                   Sat Aug 26 10:30:45 PDT 1989
(PSUVAX1) - #USENET
(PSUVAX1) - #
(PSUVAX1) - 6sigma2 thebes(DIRECT)
(PSUVAX1) -
```

Figure 6.2 Searching for a UUCP Node from BITNET

many sites still require the *node!user* syntax, sometimes requiring explicit routing from one node to the next, as in *node!node!node!user*.

Until recently, *PSUVAX1* was the main BITNET-UUCP gateway for use from the United States. It is no longer used in that capacity, but it may be queried for more information about UUCP nodes. The **UUPATH** command determines if the gateway knows the path to a UUCP node, while the **UUHOSTS** command returns everything known about a UUCP node. Commands may be sent using **SEND**:

```
SEND @PSUVAX1 UUPATH node
SEND @PSUVAX1 UUHOSTS node
```

Figure 6.2 shows the *PSUVAX1* gateway being queried for information about the UUCP *6sigma2* node. Although UUCP node names are case-sensitive, the *PSUVAX1* gateway is not.

UUCP and VMSmail

The VMS operating system interprets anything appearing on a line after an exclamation point (!) as a comment, including the exclamation point. Thus, any UUCP address must appear inside quotes, even when using **VMSmail** or **gMail**. **VMSmail** may be sent to a gateway *MAILER@UUCPGATE*, which redistributes the mail to UUCP. If explicit (*node!user*) syntax is used, the address is specified as follows:

```
To: BITNET%"node!user%MAILER@UUCPGATE"
```

If implicit (*user@node*) syntax is used, the first at (@) sign inside the quotes must be changed to a percent sign:

```
To: BITNET%"user%node%MAILER@UUCPGATE"
```

If two at (@) signs were used, gateway software might get confused as to where to send the mail.

6.3.2

UUNET

UUNET is a commercial UNIX and Usenet venture founded by the UNIX Technical User's Group (USENIX) to distribute Usenet news. [4]

Information is available on-line from *!usenix!uunet-request.*

6.4

Other Networks

Two other networks are in widespread use in the United States: CompuServe and FidoNet. CompuServe is not a network in the usual sense of having many nodes. The people using CompuServe access it via dial-up phone lines from personal computers, which may be running almost any terminal emulation software, but the personal computers are not identified by node names and are not known as nodes. Even so, CompuServe has over 500,000 subscribers, making it very popular. FidoNet is one of the largest personal computer networks in the world, with thousands of nodes.

---

4. UUNET/USENIX, PO Box 2685, Fairfax, VA 22031 (703) 764-9789.

CompuServe

CompuServe Information Systems is a commercial network accessible via dial-up lines. Where most networks consist of many computers at different sites, CompuServe computers are all at one location and not identified separately to users.

CompuServe accounts are of the form *xxxxx,yyyy* where each user is identified by a five digit number and a three or four digit number, separated by a comma. Since CompuServe computers are all at one site, and are not identified as individual nodes, CompuServe can be thought of as a network with just one node.

A gateway exists between CompuServe and the Internet, thus mail can be sent to CompuServe if it is in a format recognizable by the Internet. This is done by replacing the comma in CompuServe's *xxxxx,yyyy* account numbers with a period, and using *COMPUSERVE* as a node name:

```
xxxxx.yyyy@COMPUSERVE.COM
```

From **VMSmail**, CompuServe would be addressed as any other Internet node:

```
To: JNET%"xxxx.yyyyy@COMPUSERVE.COM"
```

CompuServe users have access to **EasyPlex** to send e-mail to other networks.

6.4.2

FidoNet

FidoNet, the popular personal computer network, consists of dial-up computers all over the world, with most sites in the United States. Each night, at preset times, certain FidoNet nodes call each other to transfer mail from one system to the next. Mail delivery is slow, sometimes taking days to get across the country.

FidoNet nodes use a *zone:network/node* syntax combined with a person's first and last names. Thus, John Smith at 1:2/3 would refer to user John Smith in zone 1, network area 2, node 3. A gateway exists between the Internet and FidoNet; mail for FidoNet may be sent to the Internet if the mail is converted using this syntax:

```
first.last@Fnode.Nnetwork.Zzone.FIDONET.ORG
```

Using the John Smith example, this would be:

```
JOHN.SMITH@F3.N2.Z1.FIDONET.ORG
```

To send from **VMSmail**, the above address would be put in quotes and addressed as:

```
To: JNET%"JOHN.SMITH@F3.N2.Z1.FIDONET.ORG"
```

Chapter 7

The Future of BITNET

One of the grand challenges for technology in the coming decade is to create an electronic network linking every scholar in the world to every other scholar and to establish a knowledge-management system on the world university network.

—Kenneth M. King, EDUCOM President, 1988 [1]

BITNET is well on its way to achieving its goal of linking the world's scholars. Ten years ago, just two universities were connected via BITNET. Today, thousands of universities are connected, and BITNET is a huge success. But simply linking the universities is not enough. The communications protocols and transmission speeds that were acceptable in the early 1980s are primitive and slow compared to today's newer technology. For BITNET to succeed in the future, it must change—transmission speeds must get much faster, more functionality must be built into the network, and human-computer interfaces must improve.

---

1. Arms, Caroline, ed. *Campus Networking Strategies*. Maynard, MA.: Digital Equipment Corporation, 1988. p.viii

The BITNET II Project

BITNET was originally conceived as an affordable computer network for universities, using existing IBM software and hardware and low speed communications lines. Since then, a massive increase in computer capacities and a large decrease in computer costs have left BITNET a little behind other computer networks. Where BITNET has largely been limited to maximum transmission speeds of 9600 bits per second (bps), other networks have implemented communications links capable of transmitting millions of bits per second, with gigabit links planned. *Dynamic routing,* where messages are transmitted by alternate routes when a node or link goes down, has long been on many BITNET users' wish lists.

The BITNET II project, discussed in Chapter 1, BITNET History & Organization, promises to strengthen BITNET. By encapsulating BITNET RSCS/NJE messages in TCP/IP messages, it is possible to send BITNET messages over other networks using standard TCP/IP tools. The benefits of such an approach include better connectivity, faster data transmission speeds, dynamic routing, and lower leased line costs. The BITNET II project has resulted in software products for a variety of computers: **VMNET** for IBM VM/CMS systems, **HUJI-NJE** and **Jnet-IP** for VAX/VMS systems, and UREP-IP for UNIX systems.

One of the weaknesses of BITNET is its inability to allow users to log on to remote nodes interactively. Originally, the BITNET II project intended to change that weakness, allowing BITNET users to access interactive services on different nodes. Perhaps a future project will address this need; it is a major limitation of BITNET.

Other networks have benefited tremendously from interactive services. Nothing illustrates this quite as well as the growth of library services offered on the Internet during the last decade. Hundreds of card catalogs at university libraries around the world are now available for searching via the Internet. But in the future, there will be access to much more than card catalogs. Due to the immense amount of information in libraries, and the difficulty in keeping track of it, librarians have rapidly accepted computers. With the invention of CD-ROMs (compact disks containing text and graphics, similar to audio compact disks), publishers have made complete books, particularly reference materials such as encyclopedias and periodical indexes, available for searching via computer. As a flood of material becomes available on CD-ROM, libraries will become the hub of computer information systems on many campuses. It is expected that the interactive login capabilities now offered for searching card catalogs will also be used for displaying and searching books, a real boon for researchers needing access to more libraries.

7.2 *User Interfaces*

The lack of good software is now a major factor in limiting the spread of computers on campuses. Computer hardware has continued its thirty-year trend of decreasing in cost while increasing in computing power, but software has not kept up with hardware technological advances. It is still not possible for a beginner to sit down and use a computer without extensive training. Accessing BITNET or other networks requires still more training, which stops most computer users from ever taking advantage of a national computer network. The lack of adequate end-user software has also prevented computers from being fully integrated into many departments on campuses.

One of the major changes coming in this decade will be the implementation of standards that will allow a common user interface across different vendors' computer platforms, from microcomputers to mainframes. Which of the proposed standards will actually become widely used is still undetermined; it is likely that there will still be multiple standards, just not as many and all more flexible and powerful than the mostly single-vendor standards of the last few decades. For the foreseeable future, computer hardware will continue to increase in power and decrease in cost, but a computer interface that allows a beginner to access computers and networks without extensive training will continue to elude us. Accessing remote databases and files is something that currently has a very steep learning curve; there is much information available, but it takes a computer hacker to find it all.

BITNET's user interface varies from one computer to the next. On IBM VM/CMS mainframes, the interface is screen-oriented so an entire screen of information is presented at once. On Digital Equipment Corporation VAX computers using Jnet software, the interface is command-line driven; each command is typed a single line at a time, and messages are displayed one line at a time. In the near future, it is expected that full-screen interfaces will be common, with a mouse (a pointing device used in conjunction with a keyboard) attached to each terminal for easier selection of menu choices. Ten years from now, common access to BITNET may be through a window (similar to a box drawn on the screen). Users will have a mouse to select the remote BITNET node and then make selections from a menu on that node. Graphic interfaces, where digitized photographs and graphic images may be displayed, have also been discussed, as have handwriting and voice recognition systems. At present, BITNET interfaces are limited simply to text characters, leaving no way for people to emphasize text even with bold print, underlining, or italics. New interfaces for BITNET present many challenges for programmers because whatever is designed will have to run on many different hardware platforms yet still maintain compatibility with existing interfaces.

More dramatic computer changes are expected after the year 2000, with access to BITNET for many users through portable computers that lack not only a keyboard but also a screen. Four technology breakthroughs promise to change the way we think about computers, which will change the way we interact with them. First, storage devices are expected to shrink in size so that hundreds of megabytes of data may be stored on a device similar to a credit card. Second, voice recognition systems will advance to the stage where they can be used acceptably on portable computers, eliminating the need for a keyboard. Third, laptop computer screens will be replaced by holograms or other projection devices, allowing much better information displays. Finally, cellular modems (which allow portable computers to be used with cellular phones) and radio-band computer networks will increase in speed and decrease in price. While portable computers at the end of this century may be similar to notepads and equipped with handwriting recognition systems, portable computers a decade later may be the size of a calculator, provide access to BITNET via a cellular modem, use a voice-recognition system to accept commands, display holograms and speak to you. This kind of technology puts the entire world at your "fingertips."

7.3   *BITNET Growth*

Because BITNET is a midlevel network in the National Science Foundation's supercomputer network (NSFNET), the growth of the NSFNET may be a major boon to BITNET. The Federal High Performance Computing Program, a five-year, $1.9 billion project proposed by the Office of Science and Technology, is expected to bring millions of dollars to a National Research and Educational Network (NREN). Of that amount, $390 million is earmarked to "support communication between persons and organizations involved in open research and scholarly pursuits in the United States." Much of the remaining money is to be used to upgrade NSFNET transmission speeds to the one gigabit level by 1996; the first experimental links at this speed are planned for 1993.

BITNET appears to have a rosy future. If current growth trends continue, the number of researchers accessing BITNET may double in less than three years. As BITNET gains faster transmission speeds and software becomes easier to use and more powerful, researchers are promised better access to more data than they can imagine. But there are people still wondering what value they are getting for the dues they paid to be a member of BITNET. The answer is what this book is all about: BITNET services.

A Networking Glossary

account name   *See* user name.

address   A node name, or user name and node name, uniquely identifying a computer, or computer user and computer. *See also* BITNET address, DECnet address, FidoNet address, Internet address, UUCP address.

alias   *See* nickname.

archives   A collection of old electronic mail or files, as in mailing list archives—copies of previously sent e-mail.

argument   *See* parameter.

ARPANET   *The Advanced Research Projects Agency NETwork,* the first national computer network in the United States, funded by the Advanced Research Projects Agency, now called the *Defense Advanced Research Projects Agency* (DARPA). In 1983, ARPANET was divided into MILNET, a military network, and ARPANET, a research network. Both were a part of the Defense Data Network (DDN), and a part of the Internet, until ARPANET was phased out in 1990.

backbone   A high speed central network that links the key nodes carrying the bulk of network traffic.

batch file   A file consisting of text commands to a computer; batch files typically contain operating system commands or commands for a specific program, such as LDBASE for searching a database. *See also* CJLI, DCL.

BBS   *Bulletin Board System. See* bulletin board.

BINARY   A file class for IBM mainframes; typically an executable file or raw data, including characters that cannot be properly displayed or printed. *See also* binary format, executable file, NETDATA, PRINTER, PUNCH.

binary format   A file format consisting of all ones and zeros. Data in such a file are typically computer operating instructions or raw data to be interpreted by a program.

bit   A unit of size, the smallest possible piece of data, often thought of as either a one or a zero or as representing an on or off state. *See also* byte, bps.

BITNET   The *Because It's There NETwork,* a world-wide computer network based on RSCS/NJE protocols to support interactive messages, file transfers, and e-mail services. BITNET links over 2300 computers (mostly DEC VAX minicomputers and IBM VM/CMS mainframes) in more than 35 countries; it includes NetNorth in Canada and EARN in Europe.

BITNET address   A network address of the form user@node, such as JOE@VAXA, where JOE is the user name of a person using a computer with the node name of VAXA.

BITNIC   The *BITNET Network Information Center,* responsible for providing technical assistance to BITNET members.

BITRCV   A program used for receiving small files sent with BITSEND and correctly assembling them into one large file.

BITSEND   A program used for dividing a large file into small files and sending the pieces to a remote computer, where they may be received and reassembled using BITRCV.

block   A unit of measurement on VAX computers. One block is equal to 512 bytes, or 1/2K. File sizes are commonly measured in blocks. *See also* byte, kilobyte.

body   The portion of an e-mail note that contains the actual message or text. A header contains address and routing information.

bps   *Bits per second,* a unit of measurement concerning how much data may be transmitted over a time period. Links between computers are measured in bps; BITNET was started using 9600 bps (1200 characters per second) links between computers.

bulletin board   An electronic messaging system, similar to regular bulletin boards where messages may be posted and read.

byte   A unit of measurement, typically equal to eight bits, or a single character. For example, the letter "A" may be thought of as one byte of data represented by the eight bits 00110001. *See also* bit, block, bps, kilobyte.

CDC   *Control Data Corporation,* a manufacturer of mainframe computers.

checksum   A calculated number used to verify the correctness of data. When files are transferred between computers, it is common to use a checksum to make sure that the data sent are the same as the data received. Thus, a checksum is calculated and included with the file being transferred; when the file is received, the checksum is recalculated and compared against the one that was sent to determine if the files are the same, without having to send two files.

CJLI   *Command Job Line Interface,* a batch file processing language used by LISTSERV for processing database requests.

CMS   *Conversational Monitor System,* providing an interactive window into the VM operating system. *See also* VM.

command   An instruction to a computer. Operating system commands deal with managing the computer, such as commands that display which people are logged on or which files are in a particular directory. Other commands are often the names of programs that are loaded from disk and executed by the computer. *See also* parameter.

CompuServe   *CompuServe Information Systems* is a commercial network accessible via dial-up lines. Where most networks consist of many computers at different sites, CompuServe consists of computers at one location, not identified separately to users.

CREN   The *Corporation for Research and Educational Networking,* a nonprofit corporation that oversees BITNET via a twelve member board of trustees.

CSNET   The *Computer Science Research NETwork,* founded by a
National Science Foundation grant in 1982 to link scientists at universities around the world. CSNET merged with BITNET in 1989 and
was phased out in 1991.

database   A file or files containing information that has similar characteristics, with a fixed organization. For example, the entries for a mailing list, each with a title, author, subject, date, and text.

database server   A specialized program for searching databases and
retrieving information from them.

DCL   *Digital Command Language* is a batch programming language
consisting of operating system instructions for VAX minicomputers.
See also batch file.

DDN   The United States Government *Defense Data Network,* consisting
of ARPANET and MILNET plus several classified military networks.

DEC   *Digital Equipment Corporation,* a company well known for its
VAX minicomputers, which are widely used on BITNET. *See also*
VAX, VMS.

DECnet   Digital Equipment Corporation's proprietary network for connecting VAX minicomputers.

DECnet address   A network address of the form *node::user,* such as
VAXA::JOE, as opposed to the standard BITNET form, *user@node,*
or JOE@VAXA.

DECnet internet   A global collection of cooperatively managed, but autonomous, networks linked by DECnet. SPAN, HEPnet, and THEnet are
all examples of large DECnet networks. *See also* internet.

digest   A collections of e-mail notes combined in a single file and
distributed, either on a regular basis or after a certain amount of
e-mail has accumulated. Digests are most typically moderated, with
the moderator deciding which notes will be accepted or rejected.

domain   A grouping of like nodes capable of communicating with each
other. Domains may include one computer, or thousands. For example,
the University of Texas has nodes that are members of the Internet
.EDU domain, or educational institution domain, consisting of university computers around the world. At the same time, the University of
Texas has its own domain consisting of all the nodes at the school and
referred to as .UTEXAS.

EARN   The *European Academic Research Network,* the portion of BITNET in Europe.

EDUCOM   A consortium of 530 universities, colleges, and other institutions, plus 95 corporate associate members. EDUCOM was formed in 1964 to "facilitate the introduction, use, and management of information technologies."

electronic magazine   Electronic magazines are similar to paper magazines, except they are transmitted electronically and typically cost nothing for a subscription. They are also similar to digests, although they are published less frequently (weekly, monthly, quarterly, or at the whim of the editor), contain longer articles, and have regular columns.

electronic mail   A note transmitted via computers, typically between two or more computer users. E-mail has a special format, including a header containing information usually found a the top of a letter (such as the date, recipient's name and address, and subject) and text making up the body of the note.

e-mail   *See* electronic mail.

ESnet   *Energy Sciences network. See* HEPnet.

executable file   A set of instructions, usually in a binary format, that a computer operating system can understand. *See also* binary file.

FidoNet   A popular personal computer network, consisting of dial-up computers all over the world with most sites in the United States. Each night, at preset times, certain FidoNet nodes call each other to transfer e-mail from one system to the next.

FidoNet address   A network address of the form *first_name.last_name @zone:network/node,* such as Joe.Smith@1:2/3, which refers to user Joe Smith in zone 1, network area 2, node 3, of FidoNet.

file   A collection of data, often text created using an editor. Each file is identified by a file name, or tag assigned to identify the contents. A good analogy is with a file cabinet; each folder (file) has a label (file name) identifying its contents. *See also* batch file, binary file, executable file.

file server   A program for automatically distributing files. BITNET file servers were developed as an addition to mailing list servers to provide access to mailing list archives and to exchange files that people discussed on mailing lists. At the bare minimum, file servers have commands for getting a directory of files and for retrieving files. Most also have a mechanism for getting online help and for sending files to the server, although this often requires special privileges. Other commands are available for maintaining and updating files on the server.

file transfer   A network service allowing files to be transferred from one computer to another on a network.

flame   An e-mail message with a derogatory or strong negative tone, sent either to another person or to a mailing list.

flame war   An exchange of heated e-mail messages, typically between two or more people on a mailing list.

foreign address   A network address that is foreign to VMSmail, i.e., not a DECnet address. VMSmail cannot handle BITNET addresses directly; a mail agent must be used to send e-mail to a foreign address. *See also* mail agent.

forum   A place for people to post messages on the topic at hand. Forums are generally unmoderated and open; anyone may send a message to a mailing list and it will automatically be rebroadcast to everyone subscribing to that list, regardless of content. This is the most common type of mailing list, and the simplest to administrate, since it is fully automated.

FTP   A *File Transfer Protocol* used on computers connected to the Internet. FTP is also the name for many programs that implement the FTP protocol on different computers.

gateway   A computer that is a member of two or more networks and is capable of transferring e-mail or files between them. Gateways have e-mail addresses on both networks and forward e-mail from one network to the other.

gMail   A *gateway Mailer* for VAX computers using the VMS operating system. gMail allows the sending of e-mail notes to non-BITNET addresses via Jnet and VMSmail.

hardware   The physical computer, as opposed to *software,* the programs that control it.

header The portion of an e-mail note that contains address and routing information. Headers have required FROM:, TO:, and SUBJ: lines, plus many optional lines. The portion of an e-mail note that contains the actual message text is called the body.

HEPnet *High Energy Physics network,* a DECnet network developed in the 1980s by the United States Department of Energy to link its high energy physics laboratories (linear accelerator sites) with universities and other research sites. Other energy research disciplines, including nuclear physics and fusion, have also been recently included, bringing the number of computers linked by HEPnet to 2500. HEPnet is evolving into the *Energy Sciences network* (ESnet), which supports protocols other than DECnet.

host A synonym for node, commonly used on other networks.

ICN *International Cooperating Network,* a network with a membership agreement with BITNET, capable of sending and receiving e-mail directly, and having full access to BITNET services.

interactive messages Short BITNET messages sent between two people who are logged on at the same time. Up to 160 characters long, these messages travel very quickly through BITNET, receiving priority over file transfers because of their small size.

internet Any networks that communicate with each other using the same protocols.

Internet, The A collection of interconnected networks based on TCP/IP protocols and sharing host naming conventions. The Internet is composed of more than 800 hosts including those on the ARPANET, MILNET, and numerous local networks at universities and private companies. Network facilities include remote login, file transfer, and e-mail. BITNET, UUCP, and JANET are not a part of the Internet since they do not use TCP/IP protocols.

internet address A network address of the form *user@node.domain,* such as JOE@VAXA.UTEXAS.EDU. Internet addresses may include many domains, depending on how a site has organized its computers. *See also* domain.

Internet protocol suite The set of protocols that define computer communications for the Internet. *See also* TCP/IP.

JANET *Joint Academic NETwork,* a network linking 200 computers at universities and research institutions in Great Britain with gateways to other networks such as BITNET.

Jnet Communications software sold by Joiner Associates Inc. that emulates the IBM RSCS protocol but is used on VAX computers with the VMS operating system. Widely used on BITNET, Jnet allows VMSmail to send to BITNET sites.

K Abbreviation for **k**ilobyte.

Kermit A file transfer protocol, primarily intended for use in transferring files between microcomputers and mainframes, developed at Columbia University in 1981.

kilobyte A unit of size, exactly 1024 bytes, but often used to mean one thousand, and abbreviated K. For example, 300,000 is often written and spoken as 300K, as in a 300K file. *See also* byte.

LAN *Local Area Network,* any small network, typically linking computers in the same room or building. *See also* WAN.

LDBASE A program for VAX computers with the VMS operating system, used to type interactive commands for searching remote LISTSERV databases.

link A physical or logical connection between two or more computers.

list server *See* mailing list server or LISTSERV.

LISTSERV A multi-purpose server that combines the functions of a mailing list server, a file server, and a database server in one program. LISTSERV was originally developed by EDUCOM in the early 1980s as a mailing list server to provide e-mail distribution to people at BITNIC who had common interests.

LISTSERV PUNCH A file format similar to the IBM PUNCH format, used by LISTSERVs for sending files with lines longer than 80 characters over BITNET. *See also* LISTSERV, LPUNCH.

local node Any computer at your location connected to a network, as opposed to remote nodes, which are computers on a network at other sites. *See also* node.

logical network   Computers that are linked to each other not by physical connections or low-level communications ability, but by software, typically e-mail programs. At a minimum with a logical network, it is possible to exchange e-mail between remote systems, but the e-mail may have to go through one or more format changes to be delivered and read.

LPUNCH   A program for VAX computers with the VMS operating system, used to convert files in LISTSERV PUNCH format to plain text. *See also* LISTSERV, LISTSERV PUNCH.

LZCMP   A program that compresses and uncompresses files using the same method as the COMPRESS program used on computers with the UNIX operating system. It compresses files so that they take up less disk space and can be transmitted faster.

mail   *See* electronic mail.

mail agent   Mail agents are programs used to interpret and translate e-mail addresses and send e-mail notes. VMSmail uses mail agents because it is unable to send e-mail to BITNET, the Internet, or UUCP addresses. *See also* foreign addresses.

mailing list   A way for people with common interests to communicate via electronic mail. When an e-mail message is sent to a mailing list, it is distributed to everyone signed up to receive copies of e-mail for that particular list.

mailing list server   A program that controls the subscribing to (and signing off from) mailing lists and that redistributes e-mail sent to it to members of a particular mailing list. Also called a *list server.*

mainframe   A large and powerful computer, typically capable of supporting hundreds of simultaneous users. Computers are divided into various loosely defined categories based on processing power and number of simultaneous users supported. From largest to smallest, these are some of the many types of computers: supercomputer, mainframe, minicomputer, workstation, and microcomputer.

Matrix   A term adapted by John Quarterman (from William Gibson's science fiction novel, *Neuromancer*) to refer to all the connected computer networks in the world.

meta-network   *See* logical network.

microcomputer   A personal computer, typically supporting one user. Computers are divided into various loosely defined categories based on processing power and number of simultaneous users supported. Typical categories, from largest to smallest, are: supercomputer, mainframe, minicomputer, workstation, and microcomputer.

MILNET   The military and defense contractor portion of the Defense Data Network, split from ARPANET in 1983, also a member of the Internet.

minicomputer   A computer supporting anywhere from several users to several hundred users, larger than a microcomputer but smaller than a mainframe. Computers are divided into various loosely defined categories based on processing power and number of simultaneous users supported, listed from largest to smallest: supercomputer, mainframe, minicomputer, workstation, and microcomputer.

moderator   A person who supervises a mailing list. Some moderators allow any messages to be posted to a list, regardless of content, while others make sure that posts are confined to relevant topics.

NETDATA   A file class for IBM mainframes. *See also* BINARY, PRINTER, PUNCH.

netnews   A program for the exchange of network e-mail widely used on UNIX computers. *See also* news programs.

NetNorth   The Canadian portion of BITNET, linking Canadian universities.

NETSERV   A program written by Berthold Pasch for IBM computers with the VM/CMS operating system; it provides distributed network file and database services across all of BITNET.

network   Two or more computers linked together using the same protocol to exchange data. Networks provide services to users, such as interactive messages, file transfers, electronic mail, and remote logins. *See also* LAN, logical network, WAN.

news programs   A category of computer software for reading e-mail from mailing lists. News programs divide e-mail into categories and keep track of which notes have been read or not read by an individual.

nickname   A user-defined alias, typically including a node name and user name. For example, rather than having to remember that Joe Smith is user JS345678 on node VAXABCD, an alias called JOE could be defined as JS345678@VAXABCD and used when sending e-mail.

NJE   *See* RSCS/NJE.

NJEF   The *Network Job Entry Facility* implemented on Control Data Corporation computers to emulate IBM NJE protocols, allowing files to be transferred over BITNET using CDC computers. *See also* RSCS/NJE.

node   A computer connected to a network. Each node has a unique node name associated with it to allow e-mail to be sent to people using that computer. A computer on more than one network may have a different name on each network. For example, SWTNYSSA is the BITNET name for a computer at Southwest Texas State University, which is referred to locally and on THEnet as NYSSA. *See also* node name, user name, local node, remote node.

node name   A unique name identifying a node on a network, much as a user name identifies a user of the computer.

Notebook   A file type used to identify files containing e-mail messages on IBM mainframes.

NSF   The *National Science Foundation,* funded by the United States Government.

NSFNET   The *National Science Foundation NETwork,* created in 1986 by the NSF to link six NSF supercomputers across the United States. NSFNET now consists of a high speed backbone using multiple connections to supercomputer sites; regional networks connect to the backbone to allow researchers access to the supercomputers.

operating system   Special software used to control computer hardware, allowing peripherals (printers, disk drives, and terminals) to communicate with each other and with a central processor and memory and to be controlled by a computer user.

parameter   A word added to a command that changes the meaning or performance of the command. For example, SEND by itself works with interactive messages, but when /FILE is added to the SEND command, as in SEND/FILE, the SEND command works with files. Two other parameters are also required with SEND/FILE, the name of the file to send and the user name of the person to receive the file. A third parameter is optional, the name of the node where the receiver has an account, if the node is different than the sender's node.

PMDF   *Pascal Memo Distribution Facility,* a program for VAX computers using the VMS operating system that allows e-mail to be sent to BITNET *user@node* addresses and Internet *user@node.domain* addresses from within VMSmail.

post   To send a message to a mailing list or bulletin board.

posting   A message sent to a mailing list or a bulletin board.

PRINTER   A file class for IBM mainframes; files of this type have lines no longer than 132 characters, are suitable for printing on a line printer and may contain special printer control codes. *See also* BINARY, NETDATA, PUNCH.

program   Computer software containing instructions written using a computer language. Programs are often compiled, or converted to binary format, to create executable programs. Uncompiled programs are also called source code.

protocol   The rules defining how computers and programs communicate with each other. For example, with computer communications, at times one computer must listen to instructions, while at other times it must give instructions. A protocol determines who's allowed to talk, who must listen, and the data format, under various conditions. BITNET uses RSCS/NJE protocols, while the Internet uses TCP/IP protocols. *See also* RSCS/NJE, TCP/IP.

protocol suite   A set of related protocols. *See also* TCP/IP.

PUNCH   A file class for IBM mainframes; this class is a holdover from the days when punch cards were used with computers. Lines are limited to 80 characters, with longer records wrapped to the next line, control codes removed, and each line starting with a length count. *See also* BINARY, NETDATA, PRINTER.

RECEIVE   A program for copying a network file from a system area into a user's work area, translating it into a requested format at the same time. Used by BITNET to receive files sent with SEND.

RELAY   A distributed message server, developed to allow simultaneous (typed) conversations between groups of people on BITNET.

RELAY server   A program controlling the receiving and retransmitting of interactive messages sent by groups of people.

remote logins   The ability to login to a computer across a network, as opposed to logging in to computer at the same site.

remote node   Any computer not at your location connected to a network, as opposed to a local node, which is a computer on a network at your site. *See also* node.

RFC   *Request For Comments* are DDN documents containing proposed and accepted networking standards, used by the Internet community. Documents are identified by a sequential number scheme, with a new RFC getting the next available number, now over 1000.

root node   In a spanning tree network, the lowest level node or nodes to which other nodes connect.

rot13   A simple data encryption method where each letter in a message is rotated 13 characters, so that "a" becomes "m", "b" becomes "n", etc. Messages that a reader might consider offensive are often encrypted using this scheme, so that a reader will not be accidentally offended. A very descriptive subject line (not encrypted) is used so that someone will not decrypt the message if they think it might offend them.

RSCS/NJE   The IBM *Remote Spooling Communications Subsystem* and *Network Job Entry* protocols, forming the underlying structure for BITNET communications. These protocols are invisible to computer users but define how messages are transferred and routed from one BITNET site to another.

SEND   A Jnet program for VAX minicomputers using the VMS operating system, to transfer interactive messages and files between BITNET nodes and to send commands to remote nodes.

server   A program that provides automatic responses to remote commands. Only certain key words are recognized as commands by a server, with the type of response depending on the command sent and the type of server. *See also* LISTSERV.

site   With respect to BITNET, a single institution, such as a university. A site may have more than one computer, thus more than one node.

SMTP   *Simple Message Transfer Protocol,* the Internet standard for transfer of e-mail messages, described in RFC 821. *See also* RFC.

software   The programs that control a computer, as opposed to *hardware,* the physical computer itself.

source code   *See* program.

SPAN   The *Space Physics Analysis Network,* a DECnet network created by NASA in 1981 to connect researchers at universities with researchers and administrators at space flight centers. SPAN now includes more than 2600 computers around the world.

supercomputer The most powerful category of computers, typically used for complex scientific and mathematical calculations. Computers are divided into various loosely defined categories based on processing power and number of simultaneous users supported, listed from largest to smallest: supercomputer, mainframe, minicomputer, workstation, and microcomputer.

TCP/IP *Transmission Control Protocol/Internet Protocol,* the Internet standards for transport of network data. These protocols, and others, make up the Internet Protocol Suite, a set of specifications for the Internet.

terminal An input/output device for accessing a computer, typically with a screen display and a keyboard.

THEnet The *Texas Higher Education network,* formed 1986 to link all institutions of higher learning in Texas. THEnet is a large regional network in the United States, with over 1200 nodes, using DECnet protocols.

topology The physical or logical structure of a network, showing nodes and the links between them.

Ultrix Digital Equipment Corporation's version of the UNIX operating system for VAX minicomputers.

UNIX A minicomputer operating system, originally developed at Bell Laboratories for American Telephone and Telegraph (AT&T), but now in widespread use. UNIX is recognized by its cryptic commands and case sensitivity, but it provides much flexibility and power, running on every class of computers from microcomputers to supercomputers.

Usenet The *User's network* is the logical world-wide network of computers that run the UNIX operating system and netnews software for exchange of network e-mail. *See also* UUCP Network.

user directory server A database server that provides name and address searching, much like receiving a phone number from a directory assistance operator or looking up a phone number in the white pages.

user name The account name or number that uniquely identifies a person on a computer. BITNET requires that user names be no longer than eight characters; longer user names are often truncated, causing problems with electronic mail and interactive messages.

UUCP *Unix-to-Unix-CoPy,* a protocol and program for computers using the UNIX operating system; it allows e-mail and files to be sent to remote users, and remote logins.

UUCP address An address of the form *node!user,* such as VAXA!JOE, as opposed to the standard BITNET form, *user@node,* or JOE@VAXA. UUCP addresses often include many nodes, separated by exclamation points, which route messages by following a path through specific computers.

UUCP network The network of systems that use the UUCP protocol to transfer e-mail and files between computers.

UUNET A commercial *UNIX* and *Usenet venture,* founded by the UNIX Technical User's Group (USENIX) to distribute Usenet news.

VAX *Virtual Architecture eXtended,* a series of minicomputers supporting from one to hundreds of users at a time, made by Digital Equipment Corporation (DEC), widely used on BITNET. VAX minicomputers typically use either the VMS or Ultrix operating systems. *See also* VMS, Ultrix.

VM IBM's proprietary *Virtual Machine* operating system, allowing IBM mainframe computer users access to their own virtual mainframe. *See also* CMS.

VMNET Programs developed by Princeton University for IBM mainframes and VAX minicomputers under the BITNET II project. VMNET encapsulates RSCS/NJE data so that it may be transferred over TCP/IP networks.

VMS *Virtual Memory System,* a proprietary operating system for Digital Equipment Corporation VAX minicomputers.

VMSDUMP A file class for DEC VAX minicomputers with Jnet software, permitting files with special characters and long lines to be transferred over BITNET, preserving long file names and characteristics that IBM RSCS/NJE protocols do not permit.

VMSmail Digital Equipment Corporation's widely used electronic mail program, sold with the VMS operating system for DEC VAX minicomputers. VMSmail does not support BITNET addresses of the form *user@node,* but is often interfaced with Jnet, which allows BITNET addresses to be specified as *JNET% "user@node"* or *BITNET% "user@node".*

VMSSERV A file server for DEC VAX minicomputers with the VMS operating system, similar to LISTSERV but much more limited.

VMS_SHARE   A program for DEC VAX minicomputers with the VMS operating system, which packages files for transmission over networks via electronic mail. It converts files with unprintable characters (such as tabs and escape sequences) and long lines into plain ASCII text files with lines of 79 characters or less. Files longer than 16K (31 VMS blocks) are split into multiple parts.

VNET   An IBM internal network that uses the same RSCS protocols as BITNET, with a gateway to BITNET.

WAN   *Wide Area Network,* any network that links computers and LANS at different sites.

white pages   The portion of American phone books providing an alphabetical listing of names, with addresses and phone numbers also listed, printed on off-white paper. Government listings (blue pages) are printed on blue paper, and commercial listings (yellow pages) on yellow paper. *See also* user directory server.

workstation   A small computer with enhanced capabilities, typically supporting just one user, but having the power of a minicomputer and the ability to execute more than one program at a time. Computers are divided into various loosely defined categories based on processing power and number of simultaneous users supported, listed from largest to smallest: supercomputer, mainframe, minicomputer, workstation, and microcomputer.

Appendix B

Recommended Reading

DEC VAX/VMS Systems:

Peters, James F., and Holmay, Patrick. ***Introduction to VAX/VMS***.
Maynard, MA: Digital Equipment Corporation, 1984.

Sawey, Ronald M., and Stokes, Troy T. ***A Beginner's Guide to VAX/
VMS Utilities and Applications***. Maynard, MA: Digital
Equipment Corporation, 1989.

Shah, Jay. ***VAX/VMS Concepts and Facilities***. New York: McGraw
Hill, 1991.

Networks:

Arms, Caroline, ed., ***Campus Networking Strategies***. Maynard, MA:
Digital Equipment Corporation, 1988.

Frey, Donnalyn, and Adams, Rick. ***!%@:: A Directory of Electronic
Mail Addressing and Networks***. Newton, MA: O'Reily and
Associates, 1989.

LaQuey, Tracy Lynn. ***User's Directory of Computer Networks***.
Maynard, MA: Digital Equipment Corporation, 1989.

Quarterman, John S. ***The Matrix: Computer Networks and Conferencing Worldwide***. Maynard, MA: Digital Equipment Corporation, 1990.

Todino, Grace. ***Using UUCP and Usenet***. Newton, MA: O'Reily and Associates, 1987.

Science Fiction:

Brunner, John. ***Shockwave Rider***. New York: Ballantine Books, 1975.

Gibson, William. ***Neuromancer***. New York: Ace, 1984.

Appendix C

Installing LDBASE

LDBASE is a set of programs for searching **LISTSERV** databases. It was written by Jan Paul Barends (SNAFA2@HLERUL51) of the Department of Biophysics at the State University of Leiden, The Netherlands. This appendix explains how to get **LDBASE** and install it on your computer, if it has not already been installed for you. Use of **LDBASE** is described in Chapter 5, Servers.

LDBASE may be retrieved from any **LISTSERV** node with this command:

```
SEND LISTSERV@node GET LDBASE COM
```

LDBASE must be uncompressed and installed before it is usable. It comes as a self-unpacking **VMS_SHARE** file (*see* Chapter 3, File Transfers), which creates a dozen small files the first time it is executed, as this example shows:

```
$ @LDBASE
%TPU-S-FILEIN, 34 lines read from file SYS$INPUT:.;
Unpacking BUILD.COM
Unpacking CLEANUP.COM
Unpacking DBS.FOR
Unpacking LDB.COM
Unpacking LDB.INFO
Unpacking SEND.FOR
Unpacking SMG.DEF
Unpacking STARTUP.COM
Unpacking TRAP.CSTR
Unpacking TRAP.FOR
Unpacking TRAP.INC
Unpacking TRAP.MESS
```

Some of these files must be compiled and linked before they can be executed, something that is done automatically as the second step of the installation process by using the **BUILD.COM** command file:

```
$ @BUILD
A description of the programs is in the file ldb.info.
TYPE SYS$SCRATCHPAD:[MM02885.BOOK5]LDB.INFO;3 ? [N]:  N
Delete sources? [Y],N  Y
```

A short delay occurs after **@BUILD** is typed, without any messages being displayed. If "Y" is answered to the delete sources question, the FORTRAN source code to the executable files will be erased. Unless you are a programmer and want to know more about how **LDBASE** works, these files are not needed. More information about **LDBASE** is available in the file *LDB.INFO*, which is not erased and may also be displayed during installation.

Installation should be complete at this point. These files remain:

```
STARTUP.COM;   1/3       A command file for defining LDBASE symbols
LDB.COM;1      2/3       A command file for running the LDBASE program
DBS.EXE;1      12/12     The actual LDBASE program
SEND.EXE;1     8/9       For sending messages
```

```
TRAP.EXE;1        11/12        For capturing message to a file
LDB.INFO;1        13/15        Information about LDBASE
LDBASE.COM;1      67/69        The original LDBASE file in VMS_SHAR format
```

Some of the programs included with **LDBASE** are special-purpose utilities. **TRAP** allows messages from a server to be captured into a file so that a record of your searches is maintained. **SEND** is a utility similar to the Jnet **SEND** program for sending interactive messages, but customized to work with **LDBASE**. **DBS** is the actual **LDBASE** program in executable format.

The command files included with **LDBASE** make running the program much easier. **STARTUP** defines global symbols and logical names so that **LDBASE** may be accessed from any directory. One of the symbols defined is **LDBASE**, which runs the *LDB.COM* file, which starts **TRAP** and **DBS**.

The first time **LDBASE** is run during a session, it should be started with these commands:

```
@STARTUP
LDB
```

Regular users of **LDBASE** may want to include the commands in *STARTUP.COM* in their *LOGIN.COM* file (a command file that automatically executes at login.)

Chapter 5, Servers, explains the use of **LDBASE**.

Mailing Lists

Most BITNET mailing lists (including digests and electronic magazines) are handled by **LISTSERVs** with automated subscriptions and mail redistributions. To get a current list of mailing lists known to a **LISTSERV**, send this command to the closest server:

```
SEND LISTSERV@node LIST GLOBAL
```

Subscriptions to these mailing lists are also handled by a **LISTSERV**, with this command:

```
SEND LISTSERV@node SUBSCRIBE list-name "your_name"
```

Note that subscription requests do NOT go to the mailing list itself, but to the **LISTSERV**. In fact, subscription requests may be sent to the closest **LISTSERV**, which will forward the request to the correct node.

LISTSERV Lists

This list was produced from a list provided by **LISTSERV@RICEVM1** on June 10, 1990. It does not contain names of all the lists available, just a selected few dozen, and has been edited and reordered. As lists come and go with frequency, some of these lists probably no longer exist but other new lists are now available. To keep track of new lists, subscribe to **NEWLIST@NDSUVM1**, a list that announces new lists.

Network ID	Full Address	List Subject
Arts		
ALLMUSIC	ALLMUSIC@AUVM	Discussions on all forms of music
ARTCRIT	ARTCRIT@YORKVM1	Art Criticism discussion forum
CINEMA-L	CINEMA-L@AUVM	Discussions on all forms of cinema
COMPOS	COMPOS@FINHUTC	Composing Digest
DESIGN-L	DESIGN-L@PSUVM	Basic design (art and architecture)
EMUSIC-D	EMUSIC-D@AUVM	Electronic Music Digest
FILM-L	FILM-L@VMTECMEX	Film making and reviews
FINE-ART	FINE-ART@RUTVM1	Fine-Art Forum
LITERARY	LITERARY@UCF1VM	Discussions about literature
NMUSIC-L	NMUSIC-L@NCSUVM	New music discussion
Communications		
COM-L	COM-L@ULKYVM	Communication discussion group
ESPER-L	ESPER-L@TREARN	Esperanto
GENDER	GENDER@RPIECS	Communication and gender
NIHONGO	NIHONGO@MITVMA	Japanese language discussion
WORDS-L	WORDS-L@YALEVM	English language discussion
Computers - Academic Uses		
ACADDR-L	ACADDR-L@MCGILL1	Academic Computing Centre Directors Forum
ACSOFT-L	ACSOFT-L@WUVMD	Academic software development
CONS-L	CONS-L@MCGILL1	Consultants forum
CCNEWS	CCNEWS@BITNIC	Campus Computing Newsletter Editors
CUMREC-L	CUMREC-L@NDSUVM1	Administrative computer use
Computers - Applications		
ALLIN1-L	ALLIN1-L@SBCCVM	ALL-IN-1 managers and users mailing list
AUTOCAD	AUTOCAD@OHSTVMA	Autocad discussion
CADLIST	CADLIST@FINHUTC	Computer aided design
CASE-L	CASE-L@UCCVMA	Computer Aided Software Engineering
INFO-KERMIT	I-KERMIT@CUVMA	INFO-KERMIT Digest
PCSERV-L	PCSERV-L@RPIECS	Public domain software servers
WP50-L	WP50-L@UBVM	WordPerfect Corporation products discussion

Network ID	Full Address	List Subject *(continued)*
Computers - BITNET		
APPLICAT	APPLICAT@BITNIC	Applications under BITNET
BITNEWS	BITNEWS@MBITNIC	BITNET News
EARNEWS	EARNEWS@FRMOP11	EARN News
FUTURE-L	FUTURE-L@BITNIC	BITNET futures list
GGUIDE	GGUIDE@BITNIC	BITNET User's Guide list
LIAISON	LIAISON@BITNIC	Network site liaisons
NETMONTH	NETMONTH@MARIST	NetMonth Magazine
NETNWS-L	NETNWS-L@NDSUVM1	Netnews list
NETSCOUT	NETSCOUT@VMTECMEX	BITNET/Internet scouts
NEW-LIST	NEW-LIST@NDSUVM1	New list announcements
POLICY-L	POLICY-L@BITNIC	Discussion about BITNET policies

Computers - Database Management Systems

Network ID	Full Address	List Subject
FOCUS-L	FOCUS-L@ASUACAD	FOCUS discussion
INGRES-L	INGRES-L@HDETUD1	INGRES discussion
ORACLE-L	ORACLE-L@SBCCVM	ORACLE discussion
SQL-L	SQL-L@MITVMA	SQL discussion list
DBASE-L	DBASE-L@TECMTYVM	dBase discussion
DB2-L	DB2-L@AUVM	DB2 discussion

Computers - Microcomputers

Network ID	Full Address	List Subject
386USERS	386USERS@NDSUVM1	386 computer users
ATARST-L	ATARST-L@UIUCVMD	Atari ST discussions
COCO	COCO@PUCC	Tandy Color Computer list
COMMODOR	COMMODOR@UBVM	Commodore computer discussion
DIST-MIC	DIST-MIC@RPIECS	Info-Micro mailing list
I-AMIGA	I-AMIGA@RUTVM1	Info-Amiga list
INF-Z100	INF-Z100@CLVM	Heath/Zenith Z100 mailing list
INFO-AP	INFO-APP@NDSUVM1	Info-Apple List
INFO-ATARI16	INFO-A16@MARIST	Atari-16 Discussion
INFO-ATARI8	INFO-A8@MARIST	Atari-8 Discussion
INFO-AUX	INFO-AUX@PUCC	A/UX operating system discussion
INFO-DEC	MD4J@CMUCCVMA	DEC Micro discussion
INFO-IBMPC	IBMPC-L@UBVM	Info-IBMPC Digest
INFO-MAC	INFO-MAC@RICEVM1	Info-MAC Digest
INFOCPM	INFOCPM@FINHUTC	CP/M operating system discussion

Network ID	Full Address	List Subject *(continued)*
NOVELL	NOVELL@SUVM	Novell LAN interest group
OS-2	OS-2@BLEKUL11	OS/2 operating system discussion

Computers - Minicomputers and Larger

Network ID	Full Address	List Subject
CICS-L	CICS-L@BYUVM	CICS list
CMSUG-L	CMSUG-L@UIUCVMD	CMS users group
CYBER-L	CYBER-L@BITNIC	CYBER list
HLPCMD-L	HLPCMD-L@BROWNVM	HELP commands for VM/CMS
HP3000-L	HP3000-L@UTCVM	HP-3000 systems discussion
HPMINI-L	HPMINI-L@UAFSYSB	Hewlett-Packard 9000 discussion
I-UNIX	I-UNIX@TCSVM	Info-Unix distribution list
IBM-MAIN	IBM-MAIN@RICEVM1	IBM mainframe discussion
INFO-TI	INFO-TI@FINHUTC	TI Explorer
INFO-VAX	INFO-VAX@MARIST	VAX minicomputer discussion
NEXT-L	NEXT-L@BROWNVM	NeXT computer list
SUPER-L	SUPER-L@MCGILL1	Super Computer Users Forum
UNIX-WIZ	UNIX-WIZ@NDSUVM1	Unix-Wizards mailing list
VAXTOOLS	VAXTOOLS@HEARN	VAX Toolbox Magazine

Computers - Miscellaneous

Network ID	Full Address	List Subject
CDROM-L	CDROM-L@UCCVMA	CD-ROM
COMP-SCI	COMP-SCI@TAUNIVM	Computer Science Distribution List
COMSOC-L	COMSOC-L@BYUVM	Computers and Society ARPA Digest
DIST-MDM	DIST-MDM@RPIECS	Info-MODEMS Mailing List
ETHICS-L	ETHICS-L@MARIST	Ethics in computing
FFP-L	FFP-L@UIUCVMD	File formats and protocols discussions
LASER	LASER@BNANDP11	Laser Lovers
LASER-L	LASER-L@IRLEARN	Laser printer information list
PSCRIPT	PSCRIPT@BNANDP11	Postscript forum
RISKS-L	RISKS-L@IRLEARN	Risks to public in the use of computers
VIRUS-L	VIRUS-L@LEHIIBM1	Computer virus discussion

Computers - Programming

Network ID	Full Address	List Subject
AILIST	AILIST@NDSUVM1	Artificial Intelligence List
APL-L	APL-L@UNBVM1	APL Language Discussion
ASSMPC-L	ASSMPC-L@USACHVM1	Assembly for the IBM-PC
C-L	C-L@UIUCVMD	C language discussions

Network ID	Full Address	List Subject *(continued)*
FIGI-L	FIGI-L@SCFVM	Forth Interest Group international list
INFO-ADA	INFO-ADA@NDSUVM1	Ada programming language
INFO-C	INFO-C@NDSUVM1	Info-C List
MODULA-L	MODULA-L@UIUCVMD	Modula-2 discussions
MUMPS-L	MUMPS-L@UGA	MUMPS list
PASCAL-L	PASCAL-L@UIUCVMD	Pascal discussion
PL1-L	PL1-L@UIUCVMD	PL1 discussion
SAS-L	SAS-L@MARIST	SAS(r) discussion
SIMULA	SIMULA@BITNIC	SIMULA language list
SPSSX-L	SPSSX-L@MARIST	SPSSX(r) discussion
TURBOC-L	TURBOC-L@YALEVM	Borland Turbo C discussion

Culture

Network ID	Full Address	List Subject
BALT-L	BALT-L@UBVM	Baltic Republics discussion list
CHILE-L	CHILE-L@PURCCVM	Discussion regarding Chile
CHINA-ND	CHINA-ND@KENTVM	China News Digest
HUMANIST	HUMANIST@BROWNVM	HUMANIST Discussion
INDIA-L	INDIA-L@UTARLVM1	Indian Interest Group
JAPAN-L	JAPAN-L@MITVMA	Japan - general topics discussion
MEXICO-L	MEXICO-L@TECMTYVM	Knowing Mexico: people, places, culture
POLAND-L	POLAND-L@UBVM	Discussion of Polish culture
PMC-LIST	PMC-LIST@NCSUVM	Postmodern Culture Journal
XCULT-L	XCULT-L@PSUVM	International Intercultural Newsletter

Health and Medicine

Network ID	Full Address	List Subject
AIDSNEWS	AIDSNEWS@RUTVM1	AIDS/HIV News
BIONEWS	BIONEWS@IRLEARN	BIOSCI BioNews Bulletin Board
BLIND-L	BLIND-L@UAFSYSB	Computer use by and for the blind
CANCER-L	CANCER-L@WVNVM	Cancer discussion
CLAN	CLAN@FRMOP11	Cancer Liaison and Action Network
DENTALMA	DENTALMA@UCF1VM	Dentistry related articles
DIABETES	DIABETES@IRLEARN	International Research Project on Diabetes
DIET	DIET@INDYCMS	Support and discussion of weight loss

Network ID	Full Address	**List Subject** (continued)
DRUGABUS	DRUGABUS@UMAB	Drug Abuse Education Information and Research
HEALTH-L	HEALTH-L@IRLEARN	International discussion on health research
MEDNEWS	MEDNEWS@ASUACAD	Health Info-Com Network Newsletter

Hobbies and Games

ADND-L	ADND-L@PUCC	Advanced Dungeons and Dragons
AUTORACE	AUTORACE@INDYCMS	Auto Racing discussion
BIRD_RBA	BIRD_RBA@ARIZVM1	National Birding Hotline Cooperative
CHESS-L	CHESS-L@GREARN	Chess discussion
FIREARMS	FIREARMS@UTARLVM1	Firearms discussion
FLYFISH	FLYFISH@UMAB	Fly Fishing Digest
FOLKLORE	FOLKLORE@TAMVM1	Folklore discussion
GAMES-L	GAMES-L@BROWNVM	Computer games list
HOCKEY-L	HOCKEY-L@MAINE	College hockey discussion
HORROR	HORROR@PACEVM	Horror
INFOHAMS	INFOHAMS@TAUNIVM	Ham Radio
NUTS	NUTS@FINHUTC	Traditional Nutty Stuff (Humor)
PETS-L	PETS-L@VMTECMEX	Domestic animal care and education list
PHOTO-L	PHOTO-L@BUACCA	Photography Phorum
ROOTS-L	ROOTS-L@NDSUVM1	Genealogy list
SCUBA-L	SCUBA-L@GUVM	Scuba diving discussion
SFLOVERS	SFLOVERS@RUTVM1	Science Fiction Lovers Digest
SPACE	SPACE@TCSVM	SPACE Digest
STORM-L	STORM-L@UIUCVMD	Storms and weather related info
TRAVEL-L	TRAVEL-L@TREARN	Tourism discussions

Political and Social Issues

AMNESTY	AMNESTY@JHUVM	Amnesty International list
AQUIFER	AQUIFER@IBACSATA	Pollution and groundwater recharge
BIOSPH-L	BIOSPH-L@UBVM	Biosphere, ecology discussion
DISARM-L	DISARM-L@ALBNYVM1	Disarmament discussion
ECONET	ECONET@MIAMIU	Ecological and environment issues
ENERGY-L	ENERGY-L@TAUNIVM	Energy list
POLCAN	POLCAN@YORKVM1	Canadian political science discussion
POLI-SCI	POLI-SCI@RUTVM1	Political Science Digest

Network ID	Full Address	List Subject *(continued)*
POLITICS	POLITICS@UCF1VM	Forum for the discussion of politics
RHETORIC	RHETORIC@RPIECS	Rhetoric, social movements, persuasion
TRANSIT	TRANSIT@GITVM1	Transit issues discussion

Religion

Network ID	Full Address	List Subject
BUDDHIST	BUDDHIST@JPNTOHOK	Forum on Indian and Buddhist studies
CHRISTIAN	CHRISTIA@FINHUTC	Practical Christian life
JUDAICA	JUDAICA@TAUNIVM	Judaic studies newsletter

University Departments

Network ID	Full Address	List Subject
AGRIC-L	AGRIC-L@UGA	Agriculture discussion
ANTHRO-L	ANTHRO-L@UBVM	Anthropology
CHEM-L	CHEM-L@UOGUELPH	Chemistry discussion
CIVIL-L	CIVIL-L@UNBVM1	Civil Engineering research & education
ENGLISH	ENGLISH@UTARLVM1	Dept. of English discussion
GEOGRAPH	GEOGRAPH@FINHUTC	Geography
HISTORY	HISTORY@FINHUTC	History
LAWSCH-L	LAWSCH-L@AUVM	Law School discussion
MECH-L	MECH-L@UTARLVM1	Mechanical Engineering discussion
PHILOSOP	PHILOSOP@YORKVM1	Philosophy discussion
PHYSICS	PHYSICS@MARIST	Physics discussion
PSYCH-L	PSYCH-L@WUVMD	Psychology discussion
SOCWORK	SOCWORK@UMAB	Social Work discussion

Miscellaneous

Network ID	Full Address	List Subject
BISEXU-L	BISEXU-L@BROWNVM	Bisexuality discussion
DAIRY-L	DAIRY-L@UMDD	Dairy discussion
MEDIA-L	MEDIA-L@BINGVMB	Media in education
PSI-L	PSI-L@RPIECS	Parapsychology discussion
SAFETY	SAFETY@UVMVM	Safety discussion
SKEPTIC	SKEPTIC@YORKVM1	SKEPTIC discussion group

Software Collections

Software collections are usually made up of public domain programs (free for anyone to use for any purpose) and shareware programs (the author requests a donation if you regularly use the program). In many cases, sites that have software collections also have other other interesting files, such as archives of mailing lists.

Access to software collections are via server, with many servers accepting an **INDEX** command, which returns a list of available files, and various **GET** or **SEND** commands for transferring files. Note that files in binary formats must be handled with care. (*See* Chapter 5, Servers, for examples of how to retrieve files.) These forms of file servers are common:

LISTSERVs - Since electronic mail is just a special type of file, it is not surprising that **LISTSERVs** handle other files in addition to mailing lists.

NETSERVs - Many of the files on **NETSERVs** have to do with network maintenance and other network functions, but there are often other files available.

VMSSERVs - For people at VMS/Jnet sites, getting executable VAX programs from **VMSSERV** sites is much easier than trying to deal with the IBM format files on **LISTSERVs** and **NETSERVs**.

TRICKLE servers - Non-U.S. sites have access to software from SIMTEL20, an Internet site that contains an extensive collection of PC software and back issues of many mailing lists. Nodes within the United States can get the same software from **LISTSERV@RPIECS** or **LISTSERV@NDSUVM1**, or via **BITFTP**.

BITFTP - **BITFTP** users have access to files available for **FTPing** on the Internet by using **BITFTP@PUCC**, a server that translates e-mail notes into **FTP** requests and then does remote logins.

Other servers - Some sites have developed their own software for handling index and file requests. If you are unsure how to access such a site, try sending a **HELP** command. An invalid command often provokes a response that reveals how to get help.

Most BITNET sites listed in this appendix came from Chris Condon's **BITNET.SERVERS** file, available from the BITNET Network Information Center with this command:

```
SEND LISTSERV@BITNIC GET BITNET SERVERS
```

E.1　　　*LISTSERV Sites*

Although **LISTSERVs** are more well known for their mailing list capabilities, they are also file servers, often serving as software depositories. To determine what files are available from a **LISTSERV**, use the **INDEX** command:

```
SEND LISTSERV@node INDEX filelist
```

Without specifying a **FILELIST** (subdirectory name), a top-level index (directory listing) is generated. The **GET** (or similar alternative) command may then be used to transfer files. Due to the number of various file types and ways of transferring them, a complete discussion of transferring files from **LISTSERVs** is included in Chapter 5, Servers. **LISTSERVs** accept commands via MAIL or MESSAGE.

The **LISTSERV** sites presented here came from Chris Condon's **BITNET.SERVERS** file, available from the BITNET Network Information Center with this command:

```
SEND LISTSERV@BITNIC GET BITNET SERVERS
```

LISTSERVs

Server	Site Name/FILELISTs
LISTSERV@AUVM	American University
LISTSERV@ASUACAD	Arizona State University
LISTSERV@BARILVM	Bar-Ilan University
LISTSERV@BITNIC	BITNET Network Information Center
	CCNEWS CCNEWS magazine & contributed article archive
	NETINFO BITNIC Information repository
LISTSERV@BLEKUL11	Katholieke Universiteit Leuven
LISTSERV@BNANDP11	Facultes Universitaires Notre Dame de la Paix
LISTSERV@BNLVMA	Brookhaven National Laboratory
LISTSERV@BROWNVM	Brown University
LISTSERV@BUACCA	Boston University
LISTSERV@BYUADMIN	Brigham Young University
	HELPCONV HELPCONV software package
LISTSERV@BYULIB	Brigham Young University
LISTSERV@CMUCCVMA	Carnegie-Mellon University Computation Center
	PCIP PCIP package
LISTSERV@EBOUB011	Centre d'Informatica de la Universitat de Barcelona
LISTSERV@EBOUB012	Centre d'Informatica de la Universitat de Barcelona
LISTSERV@CUNYVM	City University of New York
LISTSERV@CLVM	Clarkson University Schuler Resouces Center
LISTSERV@ICNUCEVM	CNUCE Istituto del CNR
LISTSERV@CUVMA	Columbia University
	MAILDIST Columbia MAILER Distribution
LISTSERV@IBACSATA	CSATA Centro Studi Applicazioni in Tecnologie Avanza
	CSATA List of documents available at CSATA
	CSATADOC PUBLIC DISC Localnet
LISTSERV@ECUVM1	East Carolina University
LISTSERV@FRECP11	Ecole Centrale de Paris
	LOCSOFT Software products written at FRECP11
LISTSERV@FRULM11	Ecole Normale Superieure
LISTSERV@TREARN	Ege University, Izmir, Turkey
LISTSERV@CEARN	European Organisation for Nuclear Research

Server	Site Name/FILELISTs
LISTSERV@ESOC	European Space Operations Centre
LISTSERV@GECRDVM1	General Electric Corporate R&D
LISTSERV@GITVM1	Georgia Inst of Technology
LISTSERV@DBNGMD12	GMD Bonn, Germany
LISTSERV@DEARN	GMD Bonn, Germany
	VM-UTIL VM system Utilities
LISTSERV@FINHUTC	Helsinki University of Technology
	DOCUMENT Documents, info, reports, essays, etc
	PICTURE CAE pictures & listings in many formats
	UTIL All kinds of utilities from everywhere
	VMPDSOFT Public Domain VM/SP software
LISTSERV@AWIIMC11	Institut fuer Medizinische Computerwissenschaften
LISTSERV@JHUVM	Johns Hopkins University
LISTSERV@KSUVM	Kansas State University
LISTSERV@HEARN	Katholieke Universiteit Nijmegen
	KERMIT Kermit files
	POLYMERP Polymer Physics database
LISTSERV@LEHIIBM1	Lehigh University
LISTSERV@MARIST	Marist College
	MRTOOLS Software tools
	VM-UTIL VM system Utilities
LISTSERV@MITVMA	Massachusetts Institute of Technology
LISTSERV@MCGILL1	McGill University
LISTSERV@TECMTYVM	Monterrey Institute of Technology
	VM-UTIL VM system Utilities
LISTSERV@SCFVM	NASA Space and Earth Sciences Computing Center
LISTSERV@BEARN	National Scientific Research Fund
LISTSERV@CANADA01	NetNorth Admin Centre
	REXX REXX pre-parser code
LISTSERV@ORION	NJIT Computer Conferencing Center
LISTSERV@NCSUVM	North Carolina State University
LISTSERV@NDSUVM1	North Dakota Higher Education Computer Network
	MINIX MINIX File Server
LISTSERV@OHSTVMA	Ohio State University

Server	**Site Name/FILELISTs** *(continued)*
LISTSERV@PSUVM	Pennsylvania State University
	REXXCOMP Rexx Compiler package
	RXKNET Rexx Knet Interface
LISTSERV@POLYGRAF	Polytechnic University
	REXXCOMP Rexx Compiler List
LISTSERV@PUCC	Princeton University
	COCO Tandy Color Computer files
	OS9 Tandy OS9 operating system
LISTSERV@PURCCVM	Purdue University
LISTSERV@QUCDN	Queen's University Computing Services
LISTSERV@QUEENS	Queens College of CUNY
LISTSERV@RPIECS	Rensselaer Polytechnic Institute
	PCSERV-L PC software
LISTSERV@RICE	Rice University
	MAC-ARCH Macintosh software repository
LISTSERV@RICECSVM	Rice University
LISTSERV@RITVM	Rochester Institute of Technology
LISTSERV@RUTVM1	Rutgers University
	POLYMERP Polymer Physics database
	PUBLIC Public Files-miscellaneous
LISTSERV@UKACRL	Rutherford Appleton Laboratory
LISTSERV@JPNSUT10	Science University of Tokyo
LISTSERV@JPNSUT30	Science University of Tokyo
LISTSERV@SLACVM	Stanford Linear Accelerator Center
LISTSERV@BINGVMB	State University of New York at Binghamton
LISTSERV@UBVM	State University of New York at Buffalo
	RFC Request For Comments
	VMS VAX/VMS public domain utilities
	VM-UTIL VM system Utilities
LISTSERV@SBCCVM	State University of New York at Stony Brook
LISTSERV@SUVM	Syracuse University
LISTSERV@DBOTUI11	Technical University Berlin
	M2CMS List of M2/CMS files
	INFOM2 List of files
	VMSOFT List of VMSOFT files
LISTSERV@TAUNIVM	Tel Aviv University
LISTSERV@TAMCBA	Texas A&M College of Business Administration

Server	**Site Name/FILELISTs** *(continued)*
LISTSERV@TAMVM1	Texas A&M University Computing Services Center
	CHINANET CHINANet information
	TEX TeX-related files
LISTSERV@TRINITY	Trinity University
LISTSERV@HDETUD1	TU Delft, Netherlands
	BILLING Computer resource chargeback
LISTSERV@TCSVM	Tulane University
	TCSSERVE The TCS server files
LISTSERV@NEUVM1	UNI-C Lyngby
LISTSERV@DKAUNI11	Universitaet Karlsruhe
	KOMET Files for KOMET members
LISTSERV@IRLEARN	University College Dublin
LISTSERV@AKRONVM	University of Akron
LISTSERV@UA1VM	University of Alabama
LISTSERV@ALBNYVM1	University of Albany
LISTSERV@UALTAVM	University of Alberta
LISTSERV@UAFSYSB	University of Arkansas Main Campus
LISTSERV@UCF1VM	University of Central Florida
LISTSERV@UGA	University of Georgia
	PCSOFT IBM PC Public Domain Software
LISTSERV@UGABUS	University of Georgia
LISTSERV@UOGUELPH	University of Guelph
LISTSERV@UHCCVM	University of Hawaii
LISTSERV@DHDURZ1	University of Heidelberg
	DRIVER TeX Driver Family
	TEXTOOLS TeX-Tools written from TeX-Users
LISTSERV@UIUCVMD	University of Illinois
LISTSERV@UKANVM	University of Kansas
LISTSERV@FARMNTON	University of Maine
LISTSERV@PORTLAND	University of Maine
LISTSERV@MAINE	University of Maine System
LISTSERV@UMSLVMA	University of Missouri
LISTSERV@IRISHVM	University of Notre Dame
LISTSERV@OREGON1	University of Oregon
LISTSERV@UOTTAWA	University of Ottawa
LISTSERV@UREGINA1	University of Regina
LISTSERV@USCVM	University of Southern California

Server	Site Name/FILELISTs *(continued)*
LISTSERV@UTCVM	University of Tennessee at Chattanooga UTCSERVE The UTC server files
LISTSERV@UTARLVM1	University of Texas at Arlington VM-UTIL VM system Utilities
LISTSERV@UTDALVM1	University of Texas at Dallas
LISTSERV@UTORONTO	University of Toronto Computing Services
LISTSERV@UWAVM	University of Washington
LISTSERV@WATDCS	University of Waterloo
LISTSERV@VILLVM	Villanova University
LISTSERV@VTVM1	Virginia Polytechnic
LISTSERV@VTVM2	Virginia Polytechnic
LISTSERV@WSUVM1	Washington State University, Pullman, WA
LISTSERV@WUVMD	Washington University
LISTSERV@WVNVM	West Virginia Network for Educational Telecomputing
LISTSERV@YALEVM	Yale University Computer Center

E.2   *NETSERV Sites*

NETSERV works in a similar fashion to **LISTSERV**. For a list of **NETSERV** sites, a **BITNET.SERVERS** file compiled by Chris Condon is available from the BITNET Network Information Center with this command:

```
SEND LISTSERV@BITNIC GET BITNET SERVERS
```

NETSERVs

Server	Site Name
NETSERV@AEARN	Austria EARN, Linz
NETSERV@BEARN	National Scientific Research Fund, Brussels
NETSERV@BITNIC	BITNET Network Information Center
NETSERV@CANADA01	NetNorth Admin Centre
NETSERV@CEARN	Centre Européen de Recherche Nucléaire
NETSERV@DEARN	German central node of EARN, Bonn
NETSERV@EBOUB011	Universidad de Barcelona
NETSERV@FINHUT	Helsinki University of Technology
NETSERV@FRMOP11	CNUSC, Montpellier
NETSERV@GREARN	Research Center of Crete, Heraklion
NETSERV@HEARN	Katholieke Universiteit Nijmegen

Server	Site Name *(continued)*
NETSERV@ICNUCEVM	National University, Pisa
NETSERV@IRLEARN	University College, Dublin
NETSERV@NORUNIT	University of Trondheim
NETSERV@NCSUVM	North Carolina State University
NETSERV@MARIST	Marist College
NETSERV@SEARN	Sweden EARN, Stockholm
NETSERV@TAUNIVM	Tel Aviv University
NETSERV@TCSVM	Tulane University
NETSERV@TREARN	Ege University, Izmir, Turkey
NETSERV@UALTAVM	University of Alberta
NETSERV@UCBCMSA	University of California at Berkeley
NETSERV@UICVM	University of Illinois, Chicago
NETSERV@UKACRL	Rutherford Appleton Laboratory UK EARN

E.3   *VMSSERV Sites*

VMSSERV works in a similar fashion to **LISTSERV** and **NETSERV**, but it was designed to handle requests specifically from VMS/JNET sites. For information on accessing a **VMSSERV** server, send a **HELP** command to the server. **VMSSERV** accepts commands via MAIL and MESSAGE. The **VMSSERV** sites listed here came from Chris Condon's **BITNET.SERVERS** file, available from the BITNET Network Information Center with this command:

```
SEND LISTSERV@BITNIC GET BITNET SERVERS
```

VMSSERVs

Server	Site Name
VMSSERV@UBVMSA	State University of New York, Buffalo
VMSSERV@UBVMSB	State University of New York, Buffalo
VMSSERV@UBVMSC	State University of New York, Buffalo
VMSSERV@UBVMSD	State University of New York, Buffalo
VMSSERV@SPCVXA	St. Peter's College, Jersey City, New Jersey
VMSSERV@TOWSON2	Towson State University, Towson, Maryland
VMSSERV@UOFT02	University of Toledo, Toledo, Ohio
VMSSERV@FHCRCVAX	Fred Hutchinson Cancer Research Center

TRICKLE Servers

TRICKLE servers provide directory listings and files from the most popular directories of SIMTEL20, a large Internet software repository in White Sands, New Mexico. **TRICKLE** servers exist to provide European and other overseas sites with software; people in the United States should access SIMTEL20 files from **LISTSERV@RPIECS** or **LISTSERV@NDSUVM1**, or via **BITFTP**, rather than going through an overseas **TRICKLE** server.

In the SIMTEL20 archives are programs for computers using MS-DOS, Macintosh, and UNIX operating systems, in addition to software for lesser known computers. For specific instructions on getting files, send any **TRICKLE** server the **/HELP** command. **TRICKLE** servers accept commands via MAIL, MESSAGE, and FILE.

The **TRICKLE** servers listed here came from Chris Condon's **BITNET.SERVERS** file, available from the BITNET Network Information Center with this command:

```
SEND LISTSERV@BITNIC GET BITNET SERVERS
```

TRICKLE Servers

Server	Site Name
TRICKLE@AWIWUW11	Wirtschaftsuniversitaet Wien
TRICKLE@DBOFUB11	FU Berlin Institut fuer angewandte Statistik
TRICKLE@DKTC11	Copenhagen Technical College
TRICKLE@DTUZDV1	Universitaet Tuebingen
TRICKLE@EBOUBO11	Universidad de Barcelona
TRICKLE@TREARN	Ege University, Izmir, Turkey
TRICKLE@BANUFS11	Univ. Faculteiten Sint-Ignatius te Antwerpen, Belgium
TRICKLE@IMIPOLI	Centro di Calcolo, Politecnico di Milano, Italy

BITFTP Server
BITFTP @ PUCC - Princeton University

The **BITFTP** server at Princeton University provides e-mail access to Internet sites via **FTP** (File Transfer Protocol); an e-mail note with login and download instructions for an **FTP** site may be sent to **BITFTP**, which then performs the specified logon and returns requested files. Any Internet site that is **FTP-able** may be reached through **BITFTP**, although transferring binary files across the Internet and BITNET is troublesome. To take advantage of this server requires an extensive knowledge of **FTP** and the name of one or more Internet sites that have files you need.

For **FTP** instructions, send an e-mail note or file to **BITFTP@PUCC** with **HELP** as the only word in the note. **BITFTP** accepts only e-mail and plain text files.

This listing of **ANONYMOUS FTP** sites (places where **ANONYMOUS** is the account name and any password will be accepted) came from ODIN@UCSCB.UCSC.EDU, who maintains an up-to-date and comprehensive list. The node number included in the listing may be used in place of the node name for mailers that do not recognize the node name.

FTP Sites

Node	Node Number	Comments
a.cs.uiuc.edu	128.174.5.20	TeX, dvi2ps, gif, texx2.7, amiga
accuvax.nwu.edu	129.105.49.1	PibTerm 4.1.3
ahwahnee.stanford.edu	36.56.0.208	pcip interface specs
ai.toronto.edu	128.100.1.65	SunOS4.0 SLIP beta, R3 xwebster fixes
albanycs.albany.edu	128.204.1.4	best of comp.graphics
allspice.lcs.mit.edu	18.26.0.115	RFC1056 (PCMAIL) stuff, MIT snmp
ames.arc.nasa.gov	128.102.18.3	pcrrn, gnu grep
arisia.xerox.com	13.1.100.206	lisp, tcp/ip, IDA sendmail kit
arizona.edu	128.196.6.1	Icon, SR, SBProlog languages
arthur.cs.purdue.edu	128.10.2.1	RCS, Purdue tech reports

Node	Node Number	Comments *(continued)*
athena-dist.mit.edu	18.71.0.38	Hesiod name server, Kerberos, moira
bitsy.mit.edu	18.72.0.3	mit worm paper
brownvm.brown.edu	128.148.128.40	MAC
bu-cs.bu.edu	128.197.2.1	Telecom
bu-it.bu.edu	128.197.2.40	lots of interesting things
bugs.nosc.mil	128.49.0.1	Minix
c.isi.edu	26.3.0.103	info-ibmpc (Tenex)
cadre.dsl. pittsburgh.edu	128.147.128.1	jove for the Mac
camelot.berkeley.edu	128.32.149.18	"pmake", yet another parallel make
cayuga.cs.roches- ter.edu	192.5.53.209	Xfig,LaTeX styles,Jove,NL-KR mail list
celray.cs.yale.edu	128.36.0.25	ispell, dictionary
charon.mit.edu	18.80.0.13	perl+patches, xdvi
cheddar.cs.wisc.edu	128.105.2.113	Common Lisp stuff, X11 courier fonts
cheops.cis.ohio- state.edu	128.146.8.62	comp.sources.*, alt.sources
citi.umich.edu	35.1.128.16	pathalias, (not CITI MacIP), webster
clutx.clarkson.edu	128.153.4.3	Turbo C stuff, net kit
cmx.npac.syr.edu	128.230.7.8	lots of stuff
cod.nosc.mil	128.49.16.5	birdlist, PCstuff
columbia.edu	10.3.0.89	NEST network simulation testbed
crocus.waterloo.edu	129.97.128.6	STEVIE (vi-clone) in /u/grwalter/ftp
cs.cmu.edu	128.2.222.173	screen, msdos interrupt list, zoo (in /afs/cs.cmu.edu/user/ ralf/pub)
cs.orst.edu	128.193.32.1	Xlisp
cs.rochester.edu	192.5.53.209	*see* cayuga.cs.rochester.edu
cs.utah.edu	128.110.4.21	A Tour of the Worm, amiga forth
csc.ti.com		preliminary clx document
cunixc.cc.columbia.edu	128.59.40.130	MM mailer, Kermit, CAP/KIP
cygnusx1.cs.utk.edu		GCC, MM, Scheme

Node	Node Number	Comments *(continued)*
dartvax.dartmouth.edu	129.170.16.4	??
decwrl.dec.com	128.45.1.1	no FTP; gatekeeper.dec.com
devvax.tn.cornell.edu	192.35.82.200	tn3270, gated
drizzle.cs.uoregon.edu	128.223.4.1	raytracing archive (markv)
dsrgsun.ces.cwru.edu	129.22.16.2	Minix,TOS atariST gcc from bammi
ecla.usc.edu	26.21.0.65	mg emacs
elbereth.rutgers.edu	128.6.4.61	/pub
emx.utexas.edu	128.83.1.33	/net.directory
expo.lcs.mit.edu	18.30.0.212	a home of X, portable bitmaps
f.ms.uky.edu	128.163.128.6	lots of interesting things
flash.bellcore.com	128.96.32.20	Karn's RFC & IEN coll.,latest NET bits
ftp.ncsa.uiuc.edu	128.174.20.50	NCSA Telnet source, Mathematica
gatekeeper.dec.com	128.45.9.52	X11,recipes,cron,map, Larry Wall stuff
ghostwheel.andrew. cmu.edu	128.2.35.1	Hershey fonts
giza.cis.ohio- state.edu	128.146.8.61	X11R3, PEX
gpu.utcs.toronto.edu	128.100.100.1	lots of stuff, pd ksh
grape.ecs.clarkson.edu	128.153.13.196	Opus BBS, ms-dos, graphics
gregorio.stanford.edu	36.8.0.11	vmtp-ip, ip-multicast
gtss.gatech.edu	128.61.4.1	amiga rexx stuff
hamlet.caltech.edu	192.12.19.3	Nansi (VMS)
hanauma.stanford.edu	36.51.0.16	Vplot graphical system
him1.cc.umich.edu		atari st (cd PC7:)
hipl.psych.nyu.edu	128.122.132.2	Jove in pub (v4.9 is latest)
hogg.cc.uoregon.edu	128.223.20.5	NorthWestNet site info
hotel.cis.ksu.edu	129.130.10.12	XBBS, msdos, U3G toolkit
hubcap.clemson.edu	192.5.219.1	GIF files, RFCs
husc6.harvard.edu	128.103.1.56	pcip, appleII archives, uumap copy and soon the parts of the ucb tahoe tape that are marked not-at&t
icec.andrew.cmu.edu	128.223.4.1	CMU Tutor, ICEC
ics.uci.edu	128.195.0.1	perfect hash function gen., web-to-c

Node	**Node Number**	**Comments** *(continued)*
indri.primate.wisc.edu	128.104.230.11	Macintosh Trans{Skel,Display, Edit}
ix1.cc.utexas.edu	128.83.1.21	amiga
ix2.cc.utexas.edu	128.83.1.29	amiga
iuvax.cs.indiana.edu	129.79.254.192	unix arc et al
j.cc.purdue.edu	128.210.0.3	c.s.{unix,x,amiga}, elm, uupc
jpl-devvax.jpl. nasa.gov	128.149.8.43	perl author
june.cs.washington.edu	128.95.1.4	TeXhax, dviapollo, SmallTalk, web2c
kampi.hut.fi	128.214.3.9	DES routines (unrestricted)
kolvi.hut.fi	128.214.3.7	ham radio (FINLAND)
kuhub.cc.ukans.edu	129.237.1.10	VMS news
labrea.stanford.edu	36.8.0.47	dvips, paranoia
lambda.lanl.gov	128.165.4.4	Toolpack/1 for math sw in f77
lancaster.andrew. cmu.edu	128.2.13.21	CMU PCIP,RFC1073 telnetd,RFC1048 bootp
larry.cs.washing- ton.edu	128.95.1.7	Poker
lbl-csam.arpa	128.3.254.6	*see* rtsg.ee.lbl.gov
linc.cis.upenn.edu	128.91.2.8	psfig for ditroff, TeX
llnl-winken.llnl.gov	128.115.14.1	comp.sources.misc
louie.udel.edu	128.175.1.3	net.exe, minix, NORDLINK, MH, amiga
m9-520-1.mit.edu	18.80.0.45	Xim (X image viewer)
maxwell.physics. purdue.edu	128.46.135.3	/pub/bible.tar.Z
mailrus.cc.umich.edu	35.1.1.26	this list, unix arc, apollo stuff
megaron.arizona.edu	192.12.69.1	*see* arizona.edu
mimsy.umd.edu	128.8.128.8	declarative languages bib, SLIP
monk.proteon.com		cc:mail to smtp gateway
mordred.cs.purdue.edu	128.10.2.2	X11R3
ncsuvx.ncsu.edu	128.109.153.1	Hack, Moria, Empire, Ogre
net1.ucsd.edu	128.54.0.10	macintosh (tenex)
nic.mr.net		Minnesota Regional Net traffic data

Node	Node Number	Comments *(continued)*
nic.ddn.mil	10.0.0.51	RFC, other network info in NETINFO:
nis.nsf.net	35.1.1.48	Merit info, NSFnet Link Letter
nisc.nyser.net	192.33.4.10	Nysernet, IETF, GOSIP
nl.cs.cmu.edu	128.2.222.56	Fuzzy Pixmap 0.84 in /usr/mlm/ftp
oddjob.uchicago.edu	128.135.4.2	NNTP, Sendmail, utils, Ethernet stuff
omnigate.clarkson.edu	128.153.4.2	PS maps of the Domain Name system.
parcvax.xerox.com		*see* arisia.xerox.com
panarea.usc.edu	128.125.3.54	Archive for "maps"
pawl.rpi.edu	128.113.10.2	DVI stuff, Atari ST, vi for dos
plains.nodak.edu	192.33.18.50	ASCII pics, /pub/picture
po1.andrew.cmu.edu	128.2.11.131	??
po2.andrew.cmu.edu	128.2.249.105	??
postgres.berkeley.edu		University INGRES,
prep.ai.mit.edu	128.52.32.14	GNU, MIT C Scheme, gnu e?grep
radio.astro.utoronto.ca		UFGATE, msdos, lots
rascal.ics.utexas.edu	128.83.144.1	KCL,MAXIMA,GCC-386,BoyerMoore prover
relgyro.stanford.edu	36.64.0.50	sunrast-to-pc
riacs.edu		SLIP
ringo.rutgers.edu	128.6.5.77	Omega sources
rtsg.ee.lbl.gov	128.3.254.68	flex
sally.cs.utexas.edu		networking stuff
sbcs.sunysb.edu	128.48.2.3	sun raster tools
scam.berkeley.edu	128.32.138.1	X sources, etc.
science.utah.edu	118.110.192.2	TeX things (tenex)
score.stanford.edu	36.8.0.46	TexHax, Atari (tenex)
sh.cs.net	192.31.103.3	misc
shambhala.berkeley.edu		xrn
sics.se		ham radio (SWEDEN)
simtel20.arpa	26.0.0.74	*see* wsmr-simtel20.army.mil
spam.istc.sri.com		Gnu, more
sphere.mast.ohio-state.edu	128.146.7.200	phone (with bugs fixed)

Node	**Node Number**	**Comments** (continued)
squid.cs.ucla.edu	128.97.16.28	soc.med.aids
sri-nic.arpa	10.0.0.51	*see* nic.ddn.mil
ssyx.ucsc.edu	128.114.133.1	atari, amiga, gifs
sumex.stanford.edu	36.44.0.6	mac archives, Mycin (SUN4), imap
sumex-2060.stanford.edu	36.45.0.87	old home of mac archives (tenex)
sun.cnuce.cnr.it		atalk, ka9q
sun.soe.clarkson.edu	128.153.12.3	Packet Driver, X11 fonts, TeX
surya.waterloo.edu	129.97.129.72	gifs, tiff format, gif2ras
stolaf.edu	130.71.128.1	news, anime, bitmaps
svax.cs.cornell.edu	128.84.254.2	TransFig, Fig-FS, NetHack
swan.ulowell.edu	129.63.224.1	sendmail, amiga, music, c.s.unix, lots
thyme.lcs.mit.edu	18.26.0.94	SUPDUP
titan.rice.edu	128.42.1.30	sun-spots, amiga ispell
tmc.edu	128.249.1.1	FUBBS bbs list
topaz.rutgers.edu	128.6.4.194	amiga
trantor.harris-atd.com	26.13.0.98	contool, chuck@%s's tools
trantor.umd.edu	128.8.1.14	Network Time Protocol(NTP), info-amiga
trwind.ind.trw.com	129.4.16.70	Turbo C src for net.exe
tumtum.cs.umd.edu	128.8.129.49	NeWS pd software
tut.cis.ohio-state.edu	128.146.8.60	GNU, lots of interesting things
ucbarpa.berkeley.edu	128.32.130.11	tn3270, pub/4.3
ucbvax.berkeley.edu	128.32.149.36	nntp, gnews, awm, empire
ucdavis.ucdavis.edu		??
ucsd.edu	128.54.16.1u	KA9Q archives, packet driver
umn-cs.cs.umn.edu	128.101.224.1	vectrex, mac, unix-pc
unmvax.unm.edu	129.24.12.128	getmaps
unocss.unl.edu	129.93.1.11	alt.sex, motss
utadnx.cc.utexas.edu	128.83.1.26	VMS sources (zetaps, laser, sxlps)
uunet.uu.net	192.12.141.129	usenet archives, much more
ux.acss.umn.edu	128.101.63.2	usenix 87 archives
uxa.cso.uiuc.edu	128.174.2.1	mac, pcsig
uxc.cso.uiuc.edu	128.174.5.50	games, misc
uxe.cso.uiuc.edu	128.174.5.54	amiga/Fish disks, PC-SIG 1-499

Node	Node Number	Comments *(continued)*
vax.ftp.com	128.127.25.100	FTP software, inc.
venera.isi.edu	128.9.0.32	statspy (NNstat)
venus.ycc.yale.edu		SBTeX
vgr.brl.mil	128.63.4.4	bsd ping + record route
venera.isi.edu	128.9.0.32	GNU Chess
watmath.waterloo.edu	129.97.128.1	lots of stuff
wsmr-simtel20.army.mil	26.0.0.74	MS-DOS, Unix, CP/M, Mac, lots! (tenex)
xanth.cs.odu.edu	128.82.8.1	c.srcs.{x,unix,misc,games, amiga},X10R4
zaphod.ncsa.uiuc.edu	128.174.20.50	NCSA Telnet source, binaries
z.andrew.cmu.edu	128.2.30.8	bugfixar + div

E.6   *Other Servers*

The servers included here came from Chris Condon's **BITNET.SERVERS** file, available from the BITNET Network Information Center with this command:

```
SEND LISTSERV@BITNIC GET BITNET SERVERS
```

Servers typically respond to a **HELP** command, which may be sent as a one line e-mail note or as an interactive message like this:

```
SEND server@node HELP
```

Remember that commands such as **HELP** should NOT be sent to mailing lists. Mailing list commands are typically sent to the **LISTSERV** that controls subscriptions and file archives. The file servers listed below do allow commands to be sent to them.

ASTRADB @ ICNUCEVM - Istituto del C.N.R, Pisa

A joint project of IBM and CNR (the Italian National Research Council), ASTRA (*Application Software and Technical Reports for Academia*) is a free European service for distributing information, public domain software, and academic project documentation. Registration is required. Once registered, ASTRA is accessible only from IBM VM mainframes.

BIOSERVE @ UMDC - University of Maryland

BIOSERVE is a file server for the biology science area, maintaining public domain Molecular Biology software and archives of more than a dozen biology-related mailing lists and digests. Commands may be sent via e-mail or interactive messages.

BITSERVE @ CUNYVM - City University of New York

BITSERVE allows access to CUNYVM CMS files and VSAM databases for general use by BITNET members. Membership lists, information on BITNET services, facilities descriptions may be obtained by searching databases. For more information, use a SEND BITSERVE INFO command instead of the usual HELP command. Commands are allowed only through interactive messages.

COMSERVE @ RPIECS - Rensselaer Polytechnic Institute

COMSERVE is a server for people interested in the study of human communications. Operated by Communications Studies assistant professors Timothy Stephen and Teresa Harrison, COMSERVE is a project of Engineering Computing Services and the departments of Language, Literature, and Communication at Rensselaer. COMSERVE maintains over 800 files, in addition to an electronic white pages, extensive mailing lists, and a bibliographic search system. Commands may be submitted via e-mail, interactive messages, and as files.

ISERVE @ UWAEE - University of Washington

ISERVE is a BITNET server for access to ISAAC, the Information System for Advanced Academic Computing. ISAAC serves as clearinghouse for information about the use of IBM PCs in higher education. To access ISERVE, you must first register; help is available by sending an e-mail note to ISAAC@UWAEE.

KERMSRV @ CUVMA - Kermit Users Server, Columbia University

KERMSRV provides access to different versions of Kermit, a free micro-mainframe communications program. A version of Kermit is available for almost every computer, including microcomputers, mini-computers, and mainframes, of all models. KERMSRV accepts commands via e-mail and interactive messages.

MACSERVE @ PUCC - Princeton University

MACSERVE maintains a depository of software for Macintosh software. Commands are allowed only via interactive messages.

RELAY Sites

RELAY is a distributed message server used for interactive communications between groups of people. Rules for accessing **RELAY** and a description of **RELAY** are included in Chapter 5, Servers, with a listing of **RELAY** nodes included here.

To find out which **RELAY** site to use, send an interactive message with a **/SERVERS** command to a nearby **RELAY** or to BITNIC:

```
SEND RELAY@BITNIC /SERVERS
```

For more information about **RELAY**, send a **/HELP** command to the **RELAY** site closest to you. This listing of **RELAY** sites came from a **BITNET.SERVERS** file edited by Chris Condon and available from **LISTSERV@BITNIC** with this command:

```
SEND LISTSERV@BITNIC GET BITNET SERVERS
```

RELAY Sites

Server	Site Name
RELAY@AEARN	Austrian EARN node at Linz
RELAY@BITNIC	BITNET Network Information Center
RELAY@CMUCCVMA	Carnegie-Mellon University
RELAY@CEARN	Centre Europeen de Recherche Nucleaire

Server	**Site Name** *(continued)*
RELAY@CLVM	Clarkson University
RELAY@UCSVM	Columbia University
RELAY@DKTC11	Copenhagen Technical College
RLY@CORNELLC	Cornell University
RELAY@DEARN	DEARN German central node of EARN at Bonn
RELAY@FRECP11	Ecole Centrale de Paris
RELAY@FRHEC11	Ecole des Hautes Etudes Commerciales
RELAY@BNANDP10	Facultés Universitaires Notre Dame de la Paix
RELAY@GITVM1	Georgia Institute of Technology
RELAY@FINHUTC	Helsinki University of Technology
RELAY@BLEKUL11	Katholieke Universiteit, Belgium
RELAY@HEARN	Katholieke Universiteit, Nijmegen
RELAY@TECMTYVM	Monterrey Institute of Technology
RELAY@BEARN	National Scientific Research Fund, Brussels, Belgium
RELAY@CANADA01	NetNorth Admin Centre
RELAY@ORION	New Jersey Institute of Technology
RELAY@NYUCCVM	New York University
RELAY@NDSUVM1	North Dakota Higher Education Computer Network
RELAY@PURCCVM	Purdue University
RELAY@JPNSUT10	Science University of Tokyo
RELAY@TAUNIVM	Tel Aviv University
RELAY@TAMVM1	Texas A&M University
RELAY@UWF	Univeristy of West Florida
RELAY@EBOUB011	Universidad Barcelona
RELAY@UALTAVM	University of Alberta
MASRELAY@UBVM	University of Buffalo
RELAY@UREGINA1	University of Regina
RELAY@UTCVM	University of Tennessee - Chattanooga
RELAY@UWAVM	University of Washington
RELAY@WATDCS	University of Waterloo
RELAY@VILLVM	Villanova University
RELAY@VTVM2	Virginia Polytechnic
RELAY@YALEVM	Yale University Computer Center
RELAY@CZHRZU1A	Zurich University

User Directory Servers

User directory servers provide "white pages" information about people using BITNET, as described in Chapter 5, Servers. In the listing below are many varieties of user directory servers, including:

NETSERVs - Usually there is one **NETSERV** per country, but seven exist for the United States, with NETSERV@BITNIC serving as the user directory server. **NETSERVs** provide user directory services on a country by country basis, allowing anyone to register.

LISTSERVs - Not all **LISTSERVs** provide user directory information, but for those that do, access is via the **/WHOIS** command.

Other servers - Some sites have developed their own user directory servers with their own unique commands for searching for names. Many user directory servers can respond to a **HELP** command, if you are not sure how to use one.

User directory servers accept either electronic mail or interactive messages, or in some cases, both. This information is included in the listing below, when it is known.

An up-to-date listing of user directory servers is included in the file **BITNET.SERVERS**, edited by Chris Condon and available from BITNIC.

To get a copy of the file, use this command:

```
SEND LISTSERV@BITNIC GET BITNET SERVERS
```

The following table was compiled from the **BITNET.SERVERS** file, with additions made for **NETSERVs**.

Server	Site	Mail or Message
LISTSERV@AUVM	American Univ.	Either
LISTSERV@BUACCA	Boston Univ.	Either
NAMESERV@BRANDEIS	Brandeis Univ.	MESSAGE
LISTSERV@CMUCCVMA	Carnegie-Mellon Univ. Computation Center	Either
LISTSERV@CEARN	Centre Européen de Recherche Nucléaire	Either
NETSERV@CEARN	Centre Européen de Recherche Nucléaire	Either
NETSERV@BITNIC	City Univ. of New York	Either
BITSERVE@CUNYVM	City Univ. of New York	MESSAGE
NETSERV@ICNUCEVM	CNUCE, Pisa, Italy	Either
NETSERV@FRMOP11	CNUSC, Montpellier, France	Either
FINGER@CUVMA	Columbia Univ.	MESSAGE
INFO@IRUCCIBM	Cork Univ.	MAIL
LISTSERV@IBACSATA	Center Studi Applic in Tec Avanzate	Either
NAMESERV@DREW	Drew Univ.	Either
LISTSERV@ESOC	European Space Operations Center	Either
NETSERV@DEARN	GMD, Bonn, Germany	Either
LISTSERV@DBNGMD12	GMD, Bonn, Germany	Either
LISTSERV@DEARN	GMD, Bonn, Germany	Either
NETSERV@SAKACS00	King Abdulaziz City for Science and Tech., Saudi Arabia	Either
LISTSERV@LEHIIBM1	Lehigh Univ.	Either
LISTSERV@MARIST	Marist College	Either
NETSERV@TECMTYVM	Monterrey Institute of Technology, Mexico	Either
LISTSERV@TECMTYVM	Monterrey Institute of Technology, Mexico	Either

Server	Site	Mail or Message *(continued)*
LISTSERV@SCFVM	NASA Space and Earth Sciences Computer Center	Either
NETSERV@BEARN	National Scientific Research Fund, Brussels, Belgium	Either
FINGER@NDSUVM1	North Dakota State Univ.	MESSAGE
IDSERVER@PSUVM	Pennsylvania State Univ.	MESSAGE
COMSERVE@RPIECS	Rensselaer Polytechnic Institute	Either
LISTSERV@RICE	Rice Univ.	Either
LISTSERV@RITVM	RITISC	Either
INFO@RITVAXD	Rochester Institute of Technology	MESSAGE
LOOKUP@RITVM	Rochester Institute of Technology	MESSAGE
NETSERV@UKACRL	Rutherford Lab, Great Britain	Either
FINGER@SPCVXA	Saint Peter's College	MESSAGE
NETSERV@JPNSUT00	Science Univ. of Tokyo	Either
LISTSERV@UBVM	State Univ. of New York - Buffalo	Either
LISTSERV@SBCCVM	State Univ. of New York - Stonybrook	Either
WHOIS@ALBNYVM1	State Univ. of New York	Either
NETSERV@IRLEARN	University College, Dublin, Ireland	Either
LISTSERV@UALTAVM	Univ. of Alberta	Either
QNAMES@BANUFS11	Univ. of Antwerp	MESSAGE
NETSERV@EBOUB011	Univ. of Barcelona, Spain	Either
NAMESERV@UNCAMULT	Univ. of Calgary	MAIL
LISTSERV@UCF1VM	Univ. of Central Florida	Either
LISTSERV@UGA	Univ. of Georgia	Either
NETSERV@FINHUT	Univ. of Helsinki, Finland	Either
NETSERV@GREARN	Univ. of Heraklion, Crete, Greece	Either
PHSERVE@UIUCVMD	Univ. of Illinois	Either
NETSERV@TREARN	Univ. of Izmir, Turkey	Either
LISTSERV@UKANVM	Univ. of Kansas	Either

Server	Site	Mail or Message *(continued)*
WHOIS@UKCC	Univ. of Kentucky	Either
NETSERV@AEARN	Univ. of Linz, Austria	Either
NETSERV@PTEARN	Univ. of Lisbon, Portugal	Either
LISTSERV@MAINE	Univ. of Maine	Either
LISTSERV@FARMNTON	Univ. of Maine, Farmington	Either
LISTSERV@PORTLAND	Univ. of Maine, Portland	Either
NETSERV@HEARN	Univ. of Nijmegen, Netherlands	Either
LISTSERV@OREGON1	Univ. of Oregon	Either
VMNAMES@UREGINA1	Univ. of Regina	MESSAGE
NETSERV@SEARN	Univ. of Stockholm, Sweden	Either
NETSERV@TAUNIVM	Univ. of Tel Aviv, Israel	Either
UTSERVER@UTKVM1	Univ. of Tennessee	MESSAGE
NETSERV@CANADA01	Univ. of Toronto, Ontario, Canada	Either
NETSERV@NORUNIT	Univ. of Trondheim, Norway	Either
VMNAMES@WEIZMANN	Weizmann Institute of Science	MESSAGE
LISTSERV@YALEVM	Yale Univ.	Either

Bibliography

Included in this bibliography are books, articles, and computer files. Some articles are also available as computer files; where possible, we've cited both sources for the infomation in one entry.

Computer files often get moved from one computer to another, even changing names in the process, but most of the files listed here are from network information centers, making them likely to be around for years to come. Many of the files listed are also available on more than one computer, although only one source has been listed for each file. Computer files are identified in the bibliography by brackets and boldface following a bibliographic entry. Because files are available through various networks, three conventions were used in identifying files:

- **[Server: LISTSERV@node, file_name file_type]** Server files are documents that are available from various BITNET servers by using the Jnet SEND command:

```
SEND LISTSERV@node GET file_name file_type
```

  LISTSERVs also respond to electronic mail messages. **RELAY** servers do not.
- **[FTP: node.domain, file_name.file_type]** Some documents are not available directly from BITNET, making the files hard to retrieve.

Many of the documents listed here are from the Internet, a
network that uses a program called **FTP** to transfer files. Internet
users often are allowed to perform remote logins to other Internet
computers for retrieving files. This process, called Anonymous
FTP, requires you to know the name of the computer to log into
(in the Internet *node.domain* format) plus the directory name and
file name of the document to retrieve. This information is provided
for BITNET users who have access to an **FTP** program; other
BITNET users may send the following command to learn more
about **FTP** and how a BITNET server, **BITFTP**, may help them
retrieve Internet files:

```
SEND BITFTP@PUCC HELP
```

Using **BITFTP** is a complicated and tedious process; documents
retrieved via **BITFTP** sometimes take days to arrive. To make the best
use of **BITFTP** requires knowing much about the Internet and about **FTP.**

- **[VMS Command: command1, command2]** Some information in this
  book came directly from on-line help commands and files. For
  users of Digital Equipment Corporation VAX minicomputers
  with Jnet, VMS commands may be typed at the VMS $ prompt.

General Information on Computers and Networks

Caroline Arms, ed. *Campus Networking Strategies.* Maynard, MA:
Digital Equipment Corporation, 1988.

Jim Cerny. "VAX/VMS Tutorial: Managing Mail." *ON-LINE*
(April/May 1998): 9–10. **[Server: LISTSERV@BITNIC, VAXMAIL CERNY_J]**

Kelly R. Conaster. "IBM Mainframe 101." *LOTUS Magazine*
(March 1990): 80–85.

Donnalyn Frey and Rick Adams. *!%@:: A Directory of Electronic
Mail Addressing and Networks.* Newton, MA: O'Reily and
Associates, 1989.

Roger W. Karraker. "Highways of the Mind." *Whole Earth Review*
(Spring 1991): 4–11.

Tracy Lynn LaQuey, ed. *User's Directory of Computer Networks.*
Maynard, MA: Digital Equipment Corporation, 1989.

Michael Miley. "The Medium Is Not The Message." *Personal
Workstation* (May 1991): 49–53.

James F. Peters and Patrick Holmay. *Introduction to VAX/VMS.* Maynard, MA: Digital Equipment Corporation, 1984.

Ivars Peterson. "Highways for Information." *Science News* 133 (June 18, 1988): 394–5.

Introduction to the IBM VM Computer. Austin: University of Texas, 1989.

John S. Quarterman and Josiah C. Hoskins. "Notable Computer Networks." *Communications of the ACM* 29, 18 (October 1986): 932–971.

John S. Quarterman. *The Matrix: Computer Networks and Conferencing Worldwide.* Maynard, MA: Digital Equipment Corporation, 1990.

Ronald M. Sawey and Troy T. Stokes. *A Beginner's Guide to VAX/VMS Utilities and Applications.* Maynard, MA: Digital Equipment Corporation, 1989.

Luisa Simone. "E-MAIL, The Global Handshake." *PC Magazine* (August 1989): 175–202.

Joseph E. St Sauver. *VAX BOOK.* University of Illinois (February 1990). **[FTP: DECOY.UOREGON.EDU, PUB/VAX.BOOK.PS]**

Daniel A. Updegrove, John A. Muffo, John A. Dunn, Jr. "Electronic Mail and Networks: New Tools for Institutional Research and University Planning." **[Server: LISTSERV@BITNIC, MAILNET UP-DEGR_D]**

Ronald F. E. Weissman. "Academic Computing: The Next Wave." **[Server: LISTSERV@BITNIC, NEXTWAVE WEISSM_R]**

BITNET

Acceptable Use Policy. Corporation for Research and Educational Networking (1990). **[Server: LISTSERV@BITNIC, CREN NET_USE]**

[e-mail collection] BITNET 2. *POLICY-L Mailing List* (November 1990). **[Server: LISTSERV@BITNIC, POLICY-L LOG9010]**

[PostScript Map of] *The BITNET Backbone, Worldwide.* Princeton University (1989). **[FTP: gatekeeper.dec.com, pub/doc/maps/letter/WORLDBONE.PS]**

[PostScript Map of] *BITNET Connectivity in North America.* Princeton University (1989). **[FTP: gatekeeper.dec.com, pub/doc/maps/letter/nalinks.ps]**

[PostScript Map of] *The BITNET/EARN Backbone.* Princeton University (1989). **[FTP: gatekeeper.dec.com, pub/doc/maps/letter/eubone.ps]**

[PostScript Map of] *BITNET Sites in North America.* Princeton University (1989). **[FTP: gatekeeper.dec.com, pub/doc/maps/letter/nabone.ps]**

Board of Trustees. Corporation for Research and Educational Networking (1989). **[Server: LISTSERV@BITNIC, CREN BOARD]**

Bylaws of the Corporation for Research and Educational Networking. Corporation for Research and Educational Networking (1989). **[Server: LISTSERV@BITNIC, CREN BYLAWS]**

James W. Cerny. *Guide to BITNET Usage for the UNH Hilbert VAX/VMS Environment.* University of New Hampshire (1987). **[Server: LISTSERV@BITNIC, BITNET_U GUIDE]**

Christopher Condon. *BITNET SERVERS.* Yale Computer Center (1989). **[Server: LISTSERV@BITNIC, BITNET SERVERS]**

Christopher Condon. *BITNET USERHELP: Still Another Version of the Completely Revised Edition.* Yale Computer Center (1989). **[Server: LISTSERV@BITNIC, BITNET USERHELP]**

A. Cohen and F. Griesen. *EARN Charter.* (1990). **[Server: LISTSERV@UKACRL, BOD30 90]**

A. Cohen. *EARN Code of Conduct.* (1990). **[Server: LISTSERV@UKACRL, BOD32 90]**

Christopher Condon, ed. [Electronic Magazine] *NETMONTH.* BITNET Services Library (August 1988). **[Server: LISTSERV@BITNIC, NETMONTH 1988AUG]**

Christopher Condon, ed. [Electronic Magazine] *NETMONTH.* BITNET Services Library (September 1988). **[Server: LISTSERV@BITNIC, NETMONTH 1988SEP]**

Christopher Condon, ed. [Electronic Magazine] *NETMONTH.* BITNET Services Library (October 1988). **[Server: LISTSERV@BITNIC, NETMONTH 1988OCT]**

Jim Conklin, ed. *Legal Aspects of International Network Communication.* Corporation for Research and Educational Networking (1990). **[Server: LISTSERV@BITNIC, LEGAL COMMERCE]**

Jim Conklin, ed. *Legal Aspects of Linking BITNET to Foreign Countries.* Corporation for Research and Educational Networking (1990). **[Server: LISTSERV@BITNIC, LEGAL COUNSEL]**

Jim Conklin, ed. *General License GTDA.* Corporation for Research and Educational Networking (1990). **[Server: LISTSERV@BITNIC, LEGAL GTDA]**

John Cox. "Joiner Updates Jnet, Plans Mail System Links." *Digital News* (January 21, 1991): 9–10.

Daniel A. Dinkin and Ronald A. Blum. *BITNET Users Guide.* Towson State University Academic Computing Service (June 1991). **[Server: LISTSERV@BITNIC, BITNET TOWSON]**

Jack Dunn. *Some Suggestions for the New Bitnet User.* Tufts University. **[Server: LISTSERV@BITNIC, BITNET DUNN_J]**

[e-mail collection] *The Fall of BITNET.* FUTURE-L Mailing List (February 1990). **[Server: LISTSERV@BITNIC, FUTURE-L LOG9002]**

Barry Finkel. *BITNET/EARN/NETNORTH Topology.* Corporation for Research and Educational Networking (1990). **[Server: LISTSERV@BITNIC, BITNET2 TOPOLOGY]**

Ned Freed. *Information About PMDF-822 V3.0.* Clearinghouse for Academic Software (1988). **[Server: LISTSERV@BITNIC, PMDF INFO]**

Ira Fuchs. "BITNET—Because It's Time." *Perspectives in Computing* 3, 1 (March 1983): 16–27.

James A. Gerland. *A User's Guide to Electronic Communications at SUNY/Buffalo.* State University of New York at Buffalo (1989). **[Server: LISTSERV@BITNIC, SUNY_U DOC]**

James A. Gerland. *A User's Guide to VMSSERV.* State University of New York at Buffalo (1988). **[Server: VMSSERV@UBVMS, VMSSERV.DOC]**

Martin Glick. "Integrating Computers into Higher Education." *EDUCOM Review* 25, 2 (Summer 1990). **[Server: LISTSERV@BITNIC, EDCOMP GLICK_M]**

Jnet Manager's Guide, 4th ed. Madison: Joiner Associates, Inc., 1988.

Jnet User's Guide, 4th ed. Madison: Joiner Associates, Inc., 1988.

Jnet v3.4 Release Information. Madison: Joiner Associates, Inc., 1989. **[VMS Command: TYPE JAN_SYSTEM:JNET034.REL]**

[From the on-line VMS help for the VMS command] *MAIL.* Digital Equipment Corporation, VMS Version 5.1, (1990). **[VMS Command: MAIL, HELP]**

John W. McCredie. "BITNET's Changing Role in Higher Education." *EDUCOM Bulletin* 11 (Summer 1984) 2–5, 11.

NODES INFO1. Corporation for Research and Educational Networking (1990). **[Server: LISTSERV@BITNIC, NODES INFO1]**

[From the on-line help for the Jnet command] *RECEIVE*. Digital Equipment Corporation, VMS Version 5.1, (1990). **[VMS Command: RECEIVE, HELP]**

Relay—A Conferencing Facility. (1989). **[Server: RELAY@TECHMTYVM, /INFO]**

Relay Commands for Users. (1989). **[Server: RELAY@TECHMTYVM, /HELP]**

[From the on-line help for the Jnet command] *SEND*. Digital Equipment Corporation, VMS Version 5.1, (1990). **[VMS Command: SEND @SWTNYSSA HELP]**

Lee Varian, Peter Olenick, and Michael Gettes. "Proposal to Restructure the Network Supporting BITNET." (September 1990). **[Server: LISTSERV@BITNIC, BIT2PLAN PROPOSAL]**

National Research and Educational Network (NREN)

Charles E. Catlett. "The NSFNET: Beginnings of a National Research Internet." *Academic Computing* (January 1989): 18–21, 59–63.

Vinton G. Cerf. "Thoughts on the National Research and Educational Network." *Corporation for National Research Initiatives (CNRI)* (1990). **[FTP: nic.ddn.net, RFC:RFC-1167]**

Steve Cisler. *NREN Report.* (December 1990). **[Server: LISTSERV@UHUPVM1, PACS-L LOG9101]**

Steven P. Jobs. "The Future of Computing in Higher Education." *EDUCOM Bulletin* 22, 1 (Spring 1987). **[Server: LISTSERV@BITNIC, JOBS BULLETIN]**

"The NREN Enigma: A New National Network?" *Telecommunications* (January 1991): 13–14.

Michael Roberts. "Implementing the NREN—The Prologue is Over." *EDUCOM Review* 25, 3 (Fall 1990). **[Server: LISTSERV@BITNIC, NREN ROBERT_M]**

Susan M. Rogers. "Educational Applications of the NREN." *EDUCOM Review* 25, 2 (Summer 1990). **[Server: LISTSERV@BITNIC, NREN ROGERS_S]**

Thomas S. Valovic. "Conflict or Cooperation? NREN And US Telecom Policy." *Whole Earth Review* (Spring 1991): 12–14.

Internet

Accessing the SIMTEL20 Archives from BITNET. **[Server: LISTSERV@RPIECS, PDGET HELP]**

David H. Crocker. *Standard for the Format of ARPA Internet Text Messages.* DDN Network Information Center (1982). **[FTP: nic.ddn.net, RFC:RFC-822]**

The DDN Network Information Center (DDN). SRI International (1988). **[FTP: ftp.nisc.sri.com, NETINFO:WHAT-THE-NIC-DOES.TXT]**

Domains. *EDUCOM* (1988). **[Server: LISTSERV@BITNIC, DOMAIN GUIDE]**

Ethics and the Internet. *DDN Network Information Center* (1989). **[FTP: nic.ddn.net, RFC:RFC-1087]**

Charles L. Hedrick. *Introduction to the Internet Protocols.* Rutgers University (1987). **[FTP: cs.rutgers.edu, /runet/tcp-ip-intro.doc]**

Ed Krol. *Hitchhikers Guide to the Internet.* University of Illinois (1987). **[FTP: nic.ddn.net, RFC:RFC-1118]**

M. Lottor. *Domain Administrators Operating Guide.* DDN Network Information Center (1987). **[FTP: nic.ddn.net, RFC:RFC-1033]**

Gary Scott Malkin, April N. Marine, and Joyce K. Reynolds. *FYI on Questions and Answers: Answers to Commonly Asked 'New Internet User' Questions.* Internet Engineering Task Force, User Services Working (1990). **[FTP: nic.ddn.net, RFC:RFC-1171]**

J. Postel and J. Reynolds. *Domain Requirements.* DDN Network Information Center (1984). **[FTP: nic.ddn.net, RFC:RFC-920]**

Stahl. *Domain Administrators Guide.* DDN Network Information Center (1987). **[FTP: nic.ddn.net, RFC:RFC-1032]**

Rich Zellich. *Interest Groups List.* SRI International (1991). **[FTP: ftp.nisc.sri.com, NETINFO:INTEREST-GROUPS.TXT**

Other Networks

Philip E. Bourne. "Mailers: VMS versus ULTRIX." *DEC Professional* (February 1990): 128–132.

Tim Clark, ed. *Hints for Getting Mail Through Various Gateways To and From JANET.* University of Warwick (1990). **[Server: LISTSERV@UKACRL, MAIL-GATEWAYS.TXT]**

Tom Jennings. *FidoNet History and Operation.* (1985). **[FTP: FIDOHIST.DOC]**

Kurt Reisler. "Usenet: A Loosely Organized But Binding Network."
  Digital Review (February 12, 1990): 28.
Ben Smith. "The Unix Connection." *BYTE* (May 1989): 245–251.
Grace Todino. *Using UUCP and Usenet.* Newton, MA: O'Reily and
  Associates, 1987.
Chuq Von Rospach. *A Primer on How to Work with the Usenet
  Community.* (1989).

Miscellaneous

William Gibson. *Neuromancer.* New York: Ace, 1984.
"Major Provisions of 1986 Electronic Privacy Act." *Congressional
  Quarterly* (October 11, 1989): 2558–9.
Gene Spafford. *Dear Emily Postnews.* Purdue University (1989).
Guy Steele and Eric S. Raymond, eds. *The Jargon File.* (1990).
  [FTP: think.com, jargon.defs]

Index